UNCLE BUSH'S LIVE FUNERAL

by

Scott Seeke

Uncle Bush's Live Funeral

Copyright © 2015 Scott Seeke

Reliquary Press
400 Northridge Dr. Suite 300 Atlanta, GA 30350

www.reliquarypress.com

ISBN: 978-1-936519-26-2
Printed in the United States of America
Reliquary Press rev. date: 6/1/2015
Cover design by Bill Coffin
Cover photo by Frank Huggins

Dedication

For Beth-

All the best things in my life come from you

Chapter One

Beth's Granddaddy

"One time," said Beth's Granddaddy, "this fella came into the funeral home, and he told us he wanted to have his own funeral before he died."

We were sitting on the brick patio outside Granddaddy's home in Loudon, Tennessee, a tiny city thirty miles from Knoxville. It was September of 2000, and he was sitting in a white iron chair. Beth's grandmother, who was nicknamed Mimi, sat in a similar chair next to him. I shared the settee with Beth, whom I had married a little over a year before. Granddaddy wore a pair of navy blue slacks and a short sleeved white button down shirt. Mimi wore a red flower print dress. Across the shaded driveway, the neighbor's chain link fence held three dogs, an unknown assortment of cats, and up against it rested an enormous black pot-bellied pig named Arnold. Giant oak trees soared above us. Their leaves gently rustled in the slight breeze.

"Really?" I asked Granddaddy. The man was always telling stories, and while I usually found them interesting, this seemed incredible.

"He sure did," Granddaddy answered. Soon he was spinning a fantastic story. In 1938, the local boogeyman, a hermit named Felix "Uncle Bush" Breazeale, came out of the woods asking to have his funeral while he was still alive. He went to the lovely, classy, only-game-in-town funeral home where

Picture appears courtesy Frank Huggins, grandson of Augustus Summers

Uncle Bush - Huggins, Frank. Date unknown.

Granddaddy worked. The funeral home was owned by Mimi's father, Frank Quinn, who had agreed to put on Uncle Bush's live funeral. What really got my attention was that thousands of people had come. They had poured in from near and far, and the funeral had been the biggest thing to happen in the area since the Civil War. Granddaddy had been involved in every phase of the funeral. He had even driven the hearse, with the "corpse" sitting up front next to him. Uncle Bush had become famous for a time; the highlight was an appearance on the Ripley's Believe It or Not radio program. Yet when he finally died, only ten people came to his burial. I was enthralled.

I looked over at Beth and saw her expression. I knew that look. She was smiling and nodding, which meant that she was being polite but didn't really care. Whenever Granddaddy had a willing audience, and often when he didn't, he would spin stories. He seemed to have a story for everyone and everywhere. Mention, say, Ohio, and he would be off and running about a man he'd met from Ohio. Or about how Mimi's family came from Ohio when she was two years old, making her technically a Yankee. Grand-daddy had a story for every time, every place, and every occasion. You couldn't sit down at his house without him telling you a story, often apropos of nothing. The funeral story, the Uncle Bush story, was the best story of his life. He told it to pretty much eve-ryone. A few times he told it to local groups such as the Lion's Club. Once he told it on a Knoxville TV show. It was a story he never got tired of telling. It was a story I could tell Beth was tired of hearing.

I looked back at Granddaddy, and a thought popped into my head:

This would make a great movie.

Granddaddy moved on to other stories, but I struggled to pay attention. The story of Uncle Bush kept spinning in my mind, and I did a lot of smiling and nodding myself. Mimi was also smiling and nod-ding, but she did it because her hearing was mostly gone. At that point, she and Granddaddy had been married for sixty-five years. Both of them were short, thin, white haired, and wore glasses. Mimi's hair had thinned a bit, but Granddaddy's was still thick and parted to the side. I'm from New York, and I found Mimi and Granddaddy to be the epitome of southern gentlefolk. They were always well dressed and polite. That seemed pretty Southern to me. I could under-stand most of what they said, but not always what they meant. That also seemed pretty Southern.

After lunch was finally over, we got in the car and Beth drove us back to her mother's house. We turned left out of the driveway and the road came to a dead

end. We took a left, then a quick right over the railroad tracks and into the town square. Loudon had the
feel of a southern Lake Woebegone. Suddenly we
were transported to the 1950s. The town square was
lined with two-story storefront businesses and the
tall, majestic, brick county courthouse. Ahead rose the
bridge that crossed the wide, slow Tennessee River.
Behind us and to the sides stretched a variety of
homes ranging from 1900s brick to 1950s ranches to
dilapidated trailers.

The road to our right summed up life in Loudon.
A block down, on the right, was the house Granddaddy grew up in. Just past that, on the left, was the
nursing home he would later live in. Next door to the
nursing home, up on the hill, was the town's small
hospital, where everyone went for all but the gravest
of injuries. That was where Mimi had given birth to
her three children, Beth's mother and her Uncles
Steve and Larry. Just past that was the house Beth's
father and his brothers and sister grew up in. There
were more homes and businesses behind us and to
our left, but that one road summed up Loudon. It's
where Granddaddy lived almost all of his life.

We left Loudon by driving over the Tennessee
River on the high, wide bridge. On the other side we
entered the country. Both sides of the road were lined
with the forests and fields that cover the hills and valleys of East Tennessee. The drive made me queasy because none of the secondary roads were level or
straight. The interstates were, but the rest of the roads
were either uphill or downhill. Though Loudon lay in
the relatively flat Great Appalachian Valley[1] , it was

still in Appalachia. The roads twisted and turned too much for my weak stomach. I grew up in that same valley near Albany, New York, but I was not used to the way roads in East Tennessee crossed over and wound around the omnipresent hills. They were called hills, but they were actually long ridges. At the bottom of each steep hill was a valley with a creek or stream. If you followed those far enough, you would come to the "holler," where the hills met and the valley ended. The roadside scenery was mostly forest, occasionally broken by an eclectic assortment of farms, McMansions, and yards full of what singer Dave Wilcox called "Appalachian Mountain Roadside Art." That was a tongue-in-cheek way of describing broken down cars, refrigerators, and every other kind of yard trash. The scenery was the same in other parts of East Tennessee, minus the McMansions. This was the place Uncle Bush's family, and Beth's family, chose to settle in the late eighteenth century. That day, while Beth drove, I wasn't looking at the scenery. I was fighting my usual nausea and thinking about that old man, Bush, and his live funeral.

We visited Beth's family around Knoxville for a few more days, then returned home to Atlanta. The story of Uncle Bush stayed with me. It has never left. After a few weeks of thinking about it, I realized that there was only one way to find out if making a movie out of Bush's story was an idea worth pursuing. I had to actually talk to someone about it. The first person would need to be Beth, but I hesitated. I had been writing off and on since taking Mr. Rutherford's creative writing class in third grade, but I had never actually published anything. In 1995, I had written a first draft of a "Lord of the Rings" style fantasy novel. It spent the last ten years languishing in a drawer in my nightstand. Around that time I had also written and submitted two science fiction short stories, both of which were so summarily rejected that I gave that up forever. That was my writing career. I was afraid Beth would laugh at me. Raising the subject was harder than asking her to marry me. A week later, while she was cleaning the kitchen, I finally got the courage.

"So, I've been thinking..." I began as she scrubbed the counter.

"Yes?" She looked up at me.

"And I was thinking...that...uh...I might try and make a movie about Uncle Bush."

"OK," she said. Then she smiled and nodded.

It was not the ringing endorsement that I'd hoped for, but then again, what did she know about writing a movie? Of course, I didn't know anything about writing a movie either, but I wasn't about to let that stop me. It probably should have, but the dream of finally becoming a professional writer propelled me forward.

The next step was to consult the only person I knew who actually did know something about writing movies. I decided to pitch it to Chris Provenzano, an old college friend who just happened to be working as a screenwriter in Hollywood. At that time, Chris and I had known each other for ten years. Though we both went to Syracuse University, he had actually studied television and film writing. I, on the other hand, had studied wildlife biology at an attached State University of New York college. Chris was short and thin, with a prominent chin and thick black hair. No one could make me laugh as easily as he could. He was just getting started in Hollywood, having moved there a year before. I chose to send him an email because if he laughed, I wouldn't be able to hear it. Not only did I know Chris would be honest with me, but he'd seen me do so many stupid things in college that we would still be friends even if this was the worst movie idea ever.

A long week after I sent it, I sat at my upstairs desk, opening email. Cloudy afternoon light was fighting its way through the closed blinds. I paused when I saw that Chris had replied. I took a deep breath, moved the mouse, and slowly clicked to open his email. I exhaled as I read. Chris absolutely loved the idea.

"I'm honored that you asked me," he wrote.

Woo-hoo!

After a few more emails, we agreed that after he finished up his current television contract, we would get started writing a movie about Uncle Bush.

But first, I had to call Granddaddy.

I had known Beth for only three years, and had not spent all that much time with her family, so I still didn't know too much about Southerners. Yet somehow, I knew I had to ask Granddaddy's permission before we got serious about this movie. The next year, in 2001, I found out that my intuition had served me well. When I called him about the movie, he still had not made up his mind about whether or not I was a suitable husband for Beth. The way I found out about that was through my mom, who was in Tennessee for Beth's ordination as a Lutheran pastor (I had been ordained the month before). At the reception, Granddaddy sought out my mom.

"Your son is a fine young man," he told her.

"Thank you!" my mom replied. The next day, she mentioned it to Beth in passing. Beth's eyes lit up.

"It means he approves of you," she told me later that day.

"But I've known him for over three years!" I exclaimed. "I came and spent a week with you when your dad died, before we were even engaged, and he's only decided now that he approves of me?"

"Yes."

Maybe the call I made to Granddaddy to ask his permission to make a movie about Bush helped him make up his mind about me. It was the only time I ever called him. As soon as I mentioned my idea, I could tell he was skeptical about such a movie ever being made. That didn't bother me; I shared his skepticism. After Granddaddy had given his approval, I asked him a question. If Chris and I were going to write a movie about Bush's funeral, we needed to know why he had it.

"Do you have any idea why Bush wanted to have the funeral?" I asked.

"Well…" Granddaddy began half of his sentences with that word, then a pause. "…there were rumors of a murder."

"A murder?" This seemed too good to be true. I started to think that maybe this story would write itself.

"That was the story." Granddaddy never could answer a question directly. By then, though, I knew that if he had more to tell, he would have volunteered it without me asking.

"Do you know anyone who might know more?"

"Well…I suppose you could ask the folks at the Roane County Heritage Commission."

"Thank you, sir," I said, concluding our conversation with a polite 'sir' just to be safe.

I set out to find out why Bush had his funeral, thinking it had something to do with this murder. I had only one lead: the Roane County Heritage Commission. It was time to take a trip to Roane County, Tennessee, where Bush had lived. Loudon had once been part of Roane County, but it had split off in 1870. The new county had been called Christiana County for about a week, but it was quickly changed when the people who lived there came to their senses about what a terrible name that was. They renamed it Loudon County after local landmark Fort Loudoun, which was named after Scottish General John Campbell, Fourth Earl of Loudoun. Campbell was commander of British forces in North America during part of the French and Indian War. He was a lousy general, but he got a fort named after him anyway.[2] Loudon was the closest town to Bush's home in Cave Creek, but when the counties had split, Cave Creek had stayed in Roane. The Heritage Commission was in the Roane County seat in Kingston. Because it was the next county over from most of her family, Beth hadn't been there much. She wanted to come see it. She and I both had new jobs as pastors in the Atlanta area, and the Christmas season and start of the New Year is a busy time in church, so it wasn't until the following spring that we finally made the trip. We stayed at Beth's mom's house, and one afternoon we drove over to visit the Heritage Commission.

The weather was superb for our drive, most of which was on the interstates. We enjoyed looking out the window at the beautiful pastoral valleys and rugged, boulder lined hillsides. We even got a brief glimpse of the gorgeous spot where the Clinch River empties into the Tennessee River before both end up in the Mississippi. Just east of this confluence, we exited the interstate into Kingston, a quaint, old-fashioned town similar to Loudon. There were actually two courthouses in the center of the old Kingston town square. Both were brick with white trim and white-columned entryways. The first was built in 1854-55, and was known as the Old Roane County Courthouse. It was a two-story Georgian style brick box with white trim and a bell tower. In 1974, a new courthouse was built on the opposite side of the square and the Old Courthouse was supposed to be demolished.[3] Some citizens, led by the Heritage Commission, got together and purchased the building and refurbished it.   It had been the home of the Heritage Commission ever since.

We found the Old Courthouse and parked. I jumped out of the car. It had taken months to arrange this trip, and my adrenaline was flowing. Unfortunately, the Roane County Heritage Commission seemed like it didn't want to be found by anyone who didn't already know where it was. Finally, Beth found a tiny sign stuck in the grass. We followed it to a door around the side of the courthouse. Walking in, we saw clapboard walls lined with pictures and filing cabinets. Behind a small glass counter, a clerk would have stood, if one had been there. No one was there to help us. We started looking around as we waited for the clerk to return. Careful not to poke around too much, I paced and looked but didn't touch. And we waited.

Someone showed up ten minutes later. It was a woman in her fifties with short salt and pepper hair, glasses, and a conservative dark blue dress with flowers on it. She greeted us politely. While Beth continued looking around, I approached her.

"I was wondering if you had anything about Bush Breazeale," I asked.

"I'm sorry, we don't," she said.

Huh? According to Granddaddy, and Beth, everyone had heard about Uncle Bush.

"You don't have anything?" I asked.

"No, we don't. I am so sorry," she said with a smile.

"No newspaper articles? Old clippings?"

She smiled and nodded.

I went back over to where Beth was looking at some pictures on the wall.

"They don't have anything," I said.

"Really?"

"Really."

I could tell that Beth was as confused as I was, but at that point there was nothing we could do. We left. It was a long, quiet ride back to Beth's mother's house. About halfway back, I broke the silence.

"What just happened?" I asked.

"I just don't know," Beth replied.

My only lead had dried up, but my mother-in-law suggested the University of Tennessee's Knoxville campus, where she worked. She thought its library had old newspapers on microfilm. I called to confirm that they had the dates I needed. They actually had microfilm copies of two Knoxville newspapers, the News-Sentinel and the Knoxville Journal, which pre-dated Bush's funeral. It was a promising lead, but our schedule was almost full with visits to various members of Beth's family. I had to squeeze my trip in between family engagements, leaving me with all of forty five minutes to find whatever I could. Starting two months before the funeral, I scanned both newspapers, copying every article about Bush I could find. I worked as fast as I could, scanning and copying the Journal first, not reading anything, just trying to get as many copies as I could. After I reached the day of the funeral, I did the same with the Sentinel. Then I skimmed the weeks after the funeral in both. When my forty five minutes was up, I had read nothing but headlines, and all the button pushing had made me sweaty, but my hard work was rewarded with a thick stack of reading material. That night, after the family obligations had been satisfied, I waded in. There was a great deal of information about the funeral, and great pictures, too, all of which would be helpful in writing a movie. But strangely, neither newspaper even hinted at why Bush wanted to have his funeral. I had lots of interesting material, but still no motivation.

Soon, Chris would be wrapping up his work on a television show and beginning work on another, but he had a window in which he could come do research. We made plans for him to fly from Los Angeles to Atlanta, and then we would drive to Beth's mom's house. I would take Chris to meet Granddaddy, and we would see if we could find anyone else who might know something. I felt it was important for Chris, a New Jersey native, to get the feel of the land and its people, so I planned a visit to the Museum of Appalachia. I had been to the museum years before and had found it full of insights into life in East Tennessee.

Located in Norris, TN, north of Knoxville, and founded in the 1960's, the Museum of Appalachia was a wonderful 'living history museum of pioneer, frontier, and early mountain artifacts of mountain life in the Southern Appalachians'.[4] Almost thirty entire buildings had been transported there from all over the Appalachians, including the cabin in which Mark Twain was rumored to have been conceived, and the cabin that was Daniel Boone's home in the four episode television show "Young Dan'l Boone." Artifacts both exceptional and mundane were arranged in a walking tour of exhibits that tell the story of both day-to-day life and major events. I thought it would be a great way for Chris to get to know the people we would be writing about. Before we went, I called the founder and director, John Rice Irwin, to arrange a meeting.

"Hello, Mr. Irwin," I began, "My name is Scott Seeke, and I am calling you because I'm writing a movie about Bush Breazeale."

"I'm boycotting Hollywood," Irwin said. That seemed like an odd way to say hello.

"You are?"

"Ever since Young Dan'l Boone," he said. I did some quick math, and realized that his boycott was twenty-five years old. "We don't allow filming here anymore."

"Well, sir, we're not really at that point yet. Right now, I'm just trying to find out more about Bush."

"So you're not a producer?"

"No," I laughed. "I'm just a writer, and my writing partner and I would like to come and tour the museum. I thought I'd call ahead because I was hoping you might know something about Bush, and maybe we could meet and talk."

"Well...I might know a thing or two," Irwin said. "We've even got some Bush artifacts."

"Cool!"

"We've got a few road signs, things like that."

"I can't wait!" What a lucky break! I had seen newspaper pictures of signs that said 'Funeral This Way' with an arrow, so I assumed this was what he was talking about. Then I decided to take a chance. "One of the things we really want to know is why Bush had his funeral. I don't suppose you know anything about that?"

"Well...there were rumors." He spoke like Granddaddy.

"Rumors?"

"Of a murder." There it was again.

"A murder?"

"Rumors of one, anyway."

"But you don't know the story?"

"I don't know it myself," Irwin said, "When are you coming?"

I told him when Chris would arrive, and he agreed to meet with us then, but I could not coax anything else out of him. If he knew anything else about Bush, he wasn't going to tell me over the phone.

Chris was due to arrive in Atlanta on September 12, 2001.

The terror attacks of September 11, 2001 cancelled Chris's trip. He tried to schedule another flight, but could not find one before he had to be in Los Angeles to begin work on a television show. Chris's television schedule was such that if we did not start writing now, it would be another year before we could begin, and neither of us wanted to wait that long. Unfortunately, the story was not going to write itself. Instead, Chris and I used what little we knew, which was that Bush's funeral had been held while he was an old man, thousands of people had come, and there were rumors of a murder. We named the film Get Low, after a Southern phrase Chris had unearthed. To "get low" is to humbly come to God and ask for forgiveness. From the moment we started writing, we knew it was not the story of the real Uncle Bush. It never would be. I still wondered what had really happened, but I had to push that aside because we had work to do. Chris and I talked on the phone for hours, three and four days a week, for a year, building on the real foundation of Uncle Bush's life to create a fictional screenplay.

By the middle of 2002, Chris and I had one that we thought was fantastic. It was time to start looking for someone to produce it. Chris submitted it to the big talent agencies in Los Angeles, William Morris and Creative Artists. They weren't interested, so he kept looking. There was nothing I could do to help. Beth and I had a daughter in early 2003. Between work and parenting, I had my hands full.

Later that year, Chris's manager, Dave Ginsberg, managed to get our screenplay into the hands of Dean

Zanuck. Dean was the son of Richard Zanuck, Academy Award winning producer of "Jaws", "Driving Miss Daisy", "Cocoon", and others. Richard's father, Daryl Zanuck, was one of the founders of 20th Century Fox Studio. The Zanuck name was iconic in Hollywood, and I couldn't believe it when they called and set up a meeting with Chris and Dave. This was a tremendous opportunity, but I could not afford a last minute plane ticket to Los Angeles. Chris, with Dave's help, would have to get the Zanucks on his own.

I was sitting on my sofa in Atlanta when the phone rang, three minutes before the meeting was supposed to start. When I saw Chris's number on the caller ID, I assumed the worst. I skipped the usual greeting.

"What's up?" I asked.

"They have a Picasso," Chris answered.

"What?"

"They have a Picasso."

"That's OK, they're the Zanucks. You need to focus..."

"In the parking garage," Chris interrupted.

"Come again?"

"They have a Picasso in the parking garage." I needed a minute for this to sink in. The Zanucks...had a Picasso...in their parking garage?

"You have to focus," I told Chris. "It's just a meeting. They're just people. Now get in there and let's make this happen!" That's what I told him. What I was thinking was how out of our league we were.

Chris and Dave overcame their Picasso shock, and Dean and his brother Harrison were great. They asked us to "take it off the table." That meant that they would agree to begin development if we would agree to stop shopping it. Of course, we agreed, and just like that we had a famous production company.

Chris and I had imagined Robert Duvall playing Bush; Dean made it happen. He also got Aaron Schneider, an Oscar-winning director, and stars Sissy Spacek and Bill Murray. We were obviously thrilled to have such an incredible cast. Beth simply couldn't believe it. I could hardly believe it myself. With this much talent assembled, Dean was confident he could find a private investor so we could avoid studio interference. A year passed, but Dean had no luck. The next year, Beth and I had another baby, and there was still no investor. The year after that, she got a new job, then I did, too, but there was still no money for the movie. Throughout this time, as I rocked my children to sleep or fed them pureed bananas, I would occasionally wonder why the real Bush had his funeral. I loved our fictional story, and was very excited about the movie, but I still wondered.

In the summer of 2008, Dean found an investor. Just like that, eight years after I first had the idea, Get Low was on.

Suddenly, news was coming fast. We were shocked to find out that not only would Get Low film in Georgia, but it would film around Atlanta. We got to meet the cast, and crew, and to be on set during shooting. One night, while we were chatting with some people we knew on set, a tall man in a suit walked in.

"Hello, I'm Bill," he said, extending his hand to Beth. It was Bill Murray, taking a break from shooting.

"I'm Beth," she said. "Nice to meet you." Then Bill turned to me, and we shook hands.

"I'm Scott," I said. "So glad you're part of this." I meant it, but man, what a clumsy way to introduce myself. It was amazing how weak in the knees I was.

Shooting took less than a month - a whirlwind in Hollywood terms. As suddenly as they had arrived, everyone was gone. The cast and crew went on to other projects. Aaron and Dean went back to Los Angeles to edit, add a soundtrack, and basically spend hours and hours watching the same footage over and over to put it all together in the best way possible. It was soon announced that the world premier would be at the Toronto Film Festival on September 12, 2009. I didn't even know there was a film festival in Toronto.

"It's one of the biggest in the world!" Beth told me.

"How do you know that?" I asked.

"Because there are always pictures of it in celebrity magazines!"

It was good to know that all her years of reading "People" and "Us Weekly" had finally paid off.

During the summer, while we waited for the premier, we returned to Tennessee for a get- together with Beth's family. Beth's Uncle Steve was there. He was the middle child of Mimi and Granddaddy, younger than Beth's Uncle Larry but older than her mom. Like Granddaddy, Steve had a full head of white hair and loved to tell stories. Recently retired, Steve had finally found the time to devote to his favorite hobby: family history. He was working on a book about Sam Rayburn, a Tennessee native to whom Beth's family was distantly related, and who had served as Speaker of the United States House of Representatives longer than anyone else in history. Naturally, Steve was interested in finding out the truth behind his father's favorite story.

"Scott, how much of this movie is real?" Steve asked me.

"Not much," I admitted.

"Well...I'd sure like to know what really happened."

"I would too, but I didn't have much luck finding out."

"Let me see what I can find out," Steve offered.

Two months later, it was time for the premiere. I had been to Toronto once before, and had a blast, but we had little time to explore. The day of the premier was a blur. I'm pretty sure we ate brunch, but I can't remember where. Beth probably got a manicure, or her hair done, or something like that, but I can't remember any details of what happened that morning or afternoon. It's as if I woke up that day, and it was instantly evening, and I was sitting in my seat with the lights coming down and the film beginning.

Scene by scene, our fictional story came to life before me.

Hopefully you've had a big moment in your life, like a first kiss, or a graduation, or the birth of a child. This was one of those moments. I was deliriously happy, and at the same time I couldn't believe it was real. I watched this great movie unfold before me, and every few minutes the realization would hit that this was my movie. It was surreal and wonderful.

After the shortest one hundred minutes of my life, Get Low ended. I suppose other people might have felt pride, and I did feel a little of that, but not a lot. What I felt instead was gratitude. It was a great movie because many people had done great work. There are so many critical decisions in every movie, and I was honored to have been a small part of such an amazing collaboration. I was also filled with thanks for the two men who had started me on this journey in the first place: Granddaddy and, of course, Bush.

During the next year, Get Low screened at several film festivals. The purpose of these screenings was to build "buzz" for our July 2010 release in theaters across the United States. We also screened at several international festivals, but I only went to Sundance and Tribeca. I did interviews at film festivals, on the radio, and on television. By the time of the Q & A after the last festival screening, at Tribeca, the first question had become a familiar one.

"What was the true story that this was based on?" someone asked.

"All we know is that there was a real Bush," I began, "he had his funeral while he was still alive, thousands of people came, and there were rumors of a murder."

While that answer seemed to satisfy those who asked, it had never satisfied me. With each interview I gave, each screening I attended, that dissatisfaction grew. The more I enjoyed the Get Low experience, the more thankful I was to both Granddaddy and Bush. The problem was that I had no way to sufficiently express that thanks. I could thank producer Dean, Robert Duvall, writer Chris, and many others, and I often did. Those thanks, along with the money and the shared experience, seemed sufficient. Yet I could not find an appropriate way to thank the men who started it all, Bush and Granddaddy. My gratitude kept growing, but I had no outlet for it.

I had to find some way to thank them.

It was not until after Get Low was released, and all the interviews were over, after all the appearances were done and the dust had settled, that I figured out what I had to do. Chris and I were talking on the phone, and I was sharing all of these feelings with him, and that my own curiosity had never been satisfied.

"I just don't know what to do," I said. "Maybe I should just write a book about what really happened."

"You know what?" he told me. "I think you should."

The problem, of course, was that I had tried to find out what had really happened before, and gotten nowhere. This time, though, I had some credibility. I was now the man who had brought Bush's story to the big screen. I just had to hope that my status as a minor celebrity would be enough to grease the wheels and inspire someone in the know to talk to me about who the real Bush was, and why he had his live funeral.

Chapter Two

The Murder of Brack Smith

The first thing I did after the Get Low publicity tour ended was rest. Once I had recovered, I emailed Steve to see what he had found. When I read his email reply several days later, I almost fell out of my chair. The first place Steve had gone was the same place I had gone: the Roane County Heritage Commission. To my shock, Steve was bubbly with excitement over a treasure trove of information. They had been very kind and generous, providing him with copies of newspaper clippings, giving him access to all sorts of records, and spending quite a bit of time with him. I was flabbergasted. When I told Steve what had happened to Beth and me, he was equally flabbergasted. Here's the email he sent when I told him about our experience:

"The people who run the Heritage Commission could not be the same people you met on your notorious trip to Kingston – they are just great! I told them that you had stopped on your visit where you encountered some rude or perhaps snooty acting people. They laughed and said that it could not have been them because, 'We're the friendly type'. While I was there, a group of local ladies came by to visit and I was introduced to them and was asked to tell them about the movie. They were excited and one wrote down the name so they would not forget. I told the people that I would have to come back and they seemed genuinely pleased and suggested that I call before coming so they could have the things I need laid out for me. Now that is true hospitality!!"

Right.

What the heck had happened?

From the moment I got Steve's email, I suspected that at least part of the explanation was that I was a Yankee, while Steve was a local with impeccable credentials. After all, he and Granddaddy were Robinsons. Their ancestors had been among the earliest European settlers in Loudon. Cherokee were there first, of course, but the first Europeans arrived after the Cherokee had lost the land on the eastern side of the Tennessee River. The Blair family came and built a ferry. Next to it, the Carmichael family ran an inn. The land on the bank opposite from the Blairs and Carmichaels became available in 1819, during the Hiwassee Land sale. It was bought by William Tunnell, James Johnston and Charles McClung. They planned a town there and named it Blair's Ferry. It was renamed Loudon in 1851.[5] Thomas Robinson, Steve and Beth's ancestor, bought some of the first property in Blair's Ferry and moved there from Virginia in 1820. Robinsons had lived there ever since.

Steve was part of a family with deep East Tennessee roots. For that reason, he was trusted. Outsiders like me, on the other hand, were not trusted at all. There was an expression I heard in Loudon that "you

were a stranger for five minutes but a newcomer for
fifty years." That may have been why Steve was
helped and I was not; I will never know. As I researched this mistrust, though, I learned that one of
the main reasons for it, and for Bush's funeral, was
the Civil War.

Even before the war, East Tennesseans were not
very trusting. Many of the first European settlers in
the area were Puritans who had suffered persecution.
That mistrust worsened during and after the Civil
War, which broke out in 1861, three years before Bush
was born. Just before the attack on Fort Sumter began
the war, Tennessee had voted to remain in the Union.
Two months after, though, Tennessee seceded. It was
the last state to join the Confederacy and the first to
rejoin the Union after the war ended in 1865. Only
Virginia would have more battles fought in it. East
Tennessee changed hands five times. It was a battle-
ground state, and the consequences of those battles
can still be felt today.

Though no actual battles took place in Loudon or
Cave Creek, there was plenty of fighting. Instead of
formal armies, the conflict in Loudon and Cave Creek
was between Union and Confederate marauders col-
lectively referred to as "bushwhackers." These were
paramilitary groups whose violence persisted several
years after the war's end. Confederate bushwhackers
often came from North Carolina to take revenge on
East Tennessee for being predominantly pro-Union.
These Confederate bushwhackers plundered, pil-
laged, took revenge, and had revenge taken on them
by Union bushwhackers. Both groups often worked

with their respective armies. For instance, when Goldman Bryson, leader of a bushwhacking group known as the First Tennessee National Guard, was killed by the Confederate bushwhackers of Thomas's Legion, orders were found on his body from Union General Ambrose Burnside.[6] Because most of the damage to the pro-Union locals was done by Confederate bushwhackers from other places, East Tennesseans learned to be cautious about trusting people they didn't know.[7]

The post war years were not much better. The bushwhackers were followed by "carpetbaggers." These were wealthy Yankees who ostensibly came south to help rebuild after the war. In reality, they made fortunes by plundering desperate locals.[8] They got their name because they often carried bags made out of carpet, which were fashionable at the time. From 1861 until Reconstruction officially ended in 1877, whether they were bushwhackers or carpetbaggers, outsiders often meant trouble in East Tennessee. People learned that it was risky to trust anyone from anywhere else. That cultural memory endured long after the war ended.[9]

The Roane County Heritage Commission had shared a lot of information with Steve. Their sources had been abundant, but when Steve had asked about these rumors of a murder, all they could give him was the name and phone number of a local historian named Rick Holt. Steve visited Rick and sent me a picture of Rick in his "office." It had taken me a minute to find Rick in the picture, hidden between stacks of local history documents. His office was a small room with a desk and several filing cabinets covered with files and loose papers. All those stacks of seemingly unorganized papers were notes about local history. Obscure observations and unconnected theories covered page after intricate page, and Rick knew them all intimately. He could find anything he wanted in a matter of seconds, remembering without any method where he put specific pages. The office looked like a fire hazard, but even if it all went up in smoke, Rick had committed a lot of his information to memory. Steve was convinced that Rick's records of local history were a treasure.

"You have got to meet Rick Holt," he said.

I agreed, and set up a meeting with Rick to find out about this murder. We met for dinner at the Five Guys Burgers and Fries in Lenoir City, which was between Loudon and Knoxville in both size and geography. Rick had told me to look for his well-used pickup truck. I watched him pull in, get out, and walk across the parking lot. Rick was short, fifty-years old, and solidly built. That day he wore blue jeans, a dark t-shirt, and a baseball cap above his glasses. There were sprinkles of grey in his short black hair. We met at the door, shook hands, and said hello. I ordered a burger for myself, while Rick got a sweet tea. I shared my overflowing cup of fries with him as we talked.

During our introductory phone conversation, Rick had said in his polite, soft East Tennessee accent that there were a "few things he wanted to talk about." As a pastor, I've heard that phrase many times. I thought I was prepared for anything. Yet when Rick started telling me about his theory of the eruption of Mount Vesuvius, it took me by surprise. Rick wondered if the description of a volcano erupting in the biblical book of Revelation, written in A.D. 90, was inspired by the A.D. 79 eruption of Mount Vesuvius, which destroyed Pompeii. As my mouth gaped, Rick made his case. He thought that the Revelation account seemed to match Pliny the Younger's description of Vesuvius' eruption, and wondered what I thought of that. I had read Revelation; I even took a course on it. Yet I had forgotten there was a volcano in it. The idea that these two were connected blew me away. I told Rick that his theory sounded just fine to me, and settled into my booth. This was not the conversation, or the man, I had expected.

I soon discovered that Rick and I shared curious natures. Rick told me that he had been ordained as a Baptist minister, but he had been defrocked because of the questions he asked. They were too penetrating and the church couldn't take it. I had gotten in trouble for asking questions a few times myself. Being defrocked had not stopped his interest in religion, but that was only one of many. He had taken courses in historical archaeology at the University of Tennessee, and worked as a volunteer in local excavations. He collected old medical books, later showing me one from the 1830's. Epidemiology was of particular interest to him. A casual remark about my denomination's effort to eliminate malaria by 2015 led to a ten-minute tangent on how smallpox was eradicated. Most of Rick's diverse knowledge was self-taught. That was how he had come to learn tidbits about everything from the bible, to Roman writing, to the history of smallpox. I liked him immediately.

Over the next several years, Rick taught me a lot about Bush, and about life in East Tennessee. One of those lessons happened that night, after I returned to my mother-in-law's house. She and Beth were sitting on the couch, talking. It was late, almost ten, and I plopped down in the easy chair with a sigh. My mother-in-law knew I was researching Uncle Bush and asked with whom I had met.

"Rick Holt," I said nonchalantly.

"Rick Holt?" Beth's Mom asked, incredulous. "Rick Holt?! Does he look like Elvis Costello?" My first reaction was surprise that my mother-in-law knew who Elvis Costello was. Then I thought about it and started laughing.

"A little stockier, maybe," I agreed, "and shorter. But yeah, he does look a little like Elvis Costello." Right down to a similar style of glasses.

"Wife is Tammy?" my mother-in-law asked.

"Yep. That's him."

"Well, would you believe I taught their kids, Katy and Taylor?" she exclaimed. At the time it seemed like a crazy coincidence. As I got to know East Tennessee better, I learned that none of us should have been surprised at all.

Rick, I was delighted to learn during our long talk at Five Guys, was born and raised in Cave Creek. Since it had first been settled and named after the eponymous Cave Creek, it had changed little. The farms that dotted the high ridges on either side of the creek valley were mostly in the same places. Rick's father did not make much money as a carpenter, so like Bush, they had lived mainly off their crops. They, too, heated their house with and cooked on wood stoves. As a child, his family used an outhouse, bathed in a metal tub, slaughtered hogs, and even grew "baccer" (tobacco) for cash. The only major differences between Bush's childhood and Rick's (in the 1950's) were that the general store and ferry had closed. Other than that, Rick's family lived much as Bush had.

Rick's father had done other work to supplement his farm income, but Bush had not. Bush had not viewed farming as an occupation, like being a plumber or orthodontist. He hadn't grown a field of crops to sell for money to buy other things. Bush was a subsistence farmer. He kept himself alive by eating what he grew, with just a few cash crops for trade or sale.[10] During Bush's life, that was how most Americans lived, but it was more the case in Appalachia than any other part of the country.[11]

It was likely that about half of Bush's farm was planted with corn, often to be ground into meal and made into cornbread. In amongst the corn, farmers would plant green beans and squash in a technique called the Three Sisters.[12] Floyd Kiesler, one of the farmers Beth and I bought food from outside Atlanta, kept saying he was going to try the Three Sisters someday. According to Floyd, it was a technique that settlers learned from Native Americans. The green beans grew up the corn stalks, eliminating the need for bean poles. The beans added nitrogen to the soil, which the corn and squash needed. The squash, meanwhile, covered the ground and kept weeds from growing. It was a technique that has been used for a long time in the Americas, and almost certainly by Bush.

Bush probably also had a small vegetable garden. There he would have grown crops like peas and sweet potatoes. Fruit trees were common. So were beehives, which provided both honey and beeswax. Oats, wheat, hay, sorghum, rye, tobacco and potatoes were the most common cash crops.[13] For Rick's family, the tobacco crop paid for Christmas. For Bush, cash crops were the source of the money he needed to buy the tools and equipment to keep his farm going, so that he could survive.

By modern standards, farms in East Tennessee were not tremendously productive. Years ago, I went to an organic farmer's market in Santa Monica, California, and the produce was big and beautiful. Each eggplant, each pepper, was a perfect, enormous specimen. Even today crops like that are difficult to grow in East Tennessee. The soil's not rich enough, there's less sun and too many bugs. When compared with the Northern states, though, Tennessee was fertile land. In 1840, Tennessee led the nation in corn production. In 1850, it led the nation in hog production. The years before the Civil War were the peak years of Tennessee farming, and Tennessee was one of the nation's agricultural leaders.[14]

Though the popular image of the South is large plantations worked by slaves, this was rare in East Tennessee. Few farmers had the means to own slaves or hire others. Instead, they and their children worked the farms themselves. Bush was trained to work at an early age. His childhood and adult days were probably spent doing heavy tasks, like plowing, planting, harvesting, feeding livestock, and mending fences. Late hours of the day and nights were for mending harnesses and making clothes or shoes. Families would do this work together around a fire, talking and telling stories to pass the time. Often, these stories were from family history, local legend, or the bible.[15] The work week for Bush, and Rick's dad, was six days long. There was no time or money for vacations. The cows had to be milked whether you wanted to do it or not. In the fall, the hogs needed to be slopped (fed) three times a day whether you were sick or not. When it was time to harvest, you had to harvest or the crops went bad and the winter stores would run out too early. It was a demanding life.

Despite all this hard work, for Bush and Rick the food usually ran out in the spring, before the new crops had grown. So, in early spring they lived off the land. Rick told me about gathering and cooking modern weeds such as dandelion and burdock. Even a few poisonous plants could be eaten if properly prepared. This may sound like desperation, but Bush, Rick, and the others in their community were often only one bad crop away from the threat of starvation.

Meat had to be raised or hunted. After the 1830s, hunting was primarily a leisure activity. During the

Civil War it became a necessity for some, but after the war it declined again. Most men hunted for sport, and venison remained a popular meat throughout Bush and Rick's lives.[16] Sheep were kept for wool, mules and horses for labor, chickens for eggs, and cattle for milk and butter. Cows were slaughtered in the fall, but beef was not popular because it was difficult to preserve. Butter and eggs were not only eaten, they were often welcome barter at the store. There, the farmers would trade for things they could not make themselves, basics such as nails, salt, or shoes. One of the farmers ran the store as a side business, and anyone could drop in virtually any time to trade for essentials. He was the only person in Cave Creek with an occupation other than farming. If the local store did not have what was needed, farmers made the journey to Loudon or Kingston.

Most of the meat Bush ate came from pigs, which were popular for two main reasons. One was that they were able to survive on a varied diet. Each day during spring and summer the hogs would go off on their own to graze on wild acorns, hickory nuts, walnuts, and chestnuts. They were allowed to run free and would return at night. To protect against theft, they were given a mark such as an ear notch. A mark made the pig the legal property of the owner, and theft was a serious offense. The mark also applied to the piglets of a marked sow, which was important because of the second reason pigs were popular: they provided a lot of meat.[17] Sows in the middle of the twentieth century usually had seven piglets per litter, and one fat pig yielded well over a hundred pounds of meat.[18]

In the late fall, the pigs to be slaughtered would be brought to pens. These pens looked like small fenced mazes and can still occasionally be seen along roadsides in the south. In the pens, the hogs would be fed corn to harden their flesh. The family would slaughter as many as they needed for the next year, perhaps a half dozen. Extra meat was sold.[19] That was often the story with farmers like Bush and Rick. It was only the leftovers that could be sold or traded, and there was not much left over.

Pigs left an indelible imprint on Southern cooking. Beth had always heard the joke that every Southern recipe started, "You fry a pound of bacon…" Pretty much every vegetable Beth ate at Mimi's house had some sort of pork in it. Even Mimi's biscuits used to be made with lard; she only switched to Crisco because it became easier to find in stores.

Mimi also made amazing pork gravies, which I didn't know existed until I met Beth. As I tried each one, I came to lament those wasted years. Sausage gravy, also called sawmill gravy, was white and thick and originally made for the dogs; this was my favorite. Red eye gravy was also very good. It was deep brownish red, made from country ham - a preserved ham unique to the South and most popular in East Tennessee.

After moving to the South, I came to love pork like I had never loved another meat. Bacon became a staple item in our house, as important as eggs or butter.

We also started putting it in everything. I have never eaten anything with bacon in it and found that the bacon made it worse. My love affair with pork goes beyond bacon though. I got a smoker and learned to make barbecued pork. Where I grew up, barbecue was anything cooked on a grill. In Georgia and Tennessee, it was smoked pork shoulder, ribs or sausage. Smoking pork became one of the great joys of my life, and eating pork became a lifestyle, just like Bush's life a century before.

Though Bush's farm life seemed idyllic, he did not spend his years on the porch watching the birds go by. It was a hard life, and for that reason community was of vital importance. Having people to rely upon in tough times could be the difference between life and death. Plus other people were often the best form of entertainment. Experiencing community was made difficult by the fact that Cave Creek was a farmstead community. In a farming village, the farmers live together, but their fields are outside the village. There is no center to a farmstead community, because it is nothing more than a collection of scattered farms. I was surprised to learn that this was how most Americans lived during Bush's early life.[20] The distance between them made community even more important. I would learn just how important on the day I visited Rick's childhood home in Cave Creek.

On that day, as I looked across the valley at Rick's childhood home, birds flew past as they and the cicadas sang. Along with the wind brushing the hay in the fields, those were the only sounds. No cars could be heard passing. Despite the heat, no air-conditioners hummed. It felt like we were intruding on nature. In this place, Rick was born, raised, and became a man. At the edge of Rick's old family farmstead, where the road now runs, an old barn used to stand. This was the barn where Brack Smith was killed, and where the Civil War reared its ugly head yet again, setting the stage for Bush's live funeral.

Rick Holt pointing at family farm–
Author's collection, 2010

Rick knew the story of Brack Smith's murder well. He knew it by heart before he had ever heard of Uncle Bush or his live funeral. Over the years, he had interviewed dozens of people about it. He kept records of these conversations in the cluttered office I had seen in Steve's picture. Despite Rick's almost encyclopedic knowledge, though, very few things about the murder of Brack Smith were certain. What he did know, he was glad to share.

As dusk fell on August 6, 1891, Roane County Constable James Breckenridge "Brack" Smith returned home to Cave Creek from the county seat in Kingston. Riding in the wagon with him was James F. Littleton, a distant relative of Bush on his mother's side. The two men rode down Cave Creek Valley, past distant farmsteads where men in fields finished their day's work. They passed the store and turned off the road toward the Smith family barn. Smith's wife sent out their youngest child, eight-year-old Francis, with a lantern. She was preparing dinner, it was nearly dark, and his father would need the light to get back to the house. As the youngster walked down the hill, Smith and Littleton pushed the wagon inside the log barn alongside the road. Suddenly, a shotgun blast rang out from the cornfield across the road. As his son watched, eleven balls of buckshot shredded Brack Smith's back and left shoulder. Jim Littleton turned and saw the tassels of corn rustling as the shooter, or shooters, ran off through the cornfield into the dark.

"I'm killed," Smith cried out and, with his horrified son watching, keeled over dead. He left behind a thirty-four year old widow and four children: daughters Effa (age fourteen), Cintha (age thirteen), Lula (age eleven), and poor Francis, their only son.

The road across the valley from where Brack Smith was killed is named Harvey Road. At the time of the murder, it was the Harvey family that lived closest. According to Rick, George Harvey was talking with members of the Miller and Hall families. Gathered around a haystack, they stood at the top of the hill overlooking the scene of the murder, though it would have been invisible through the trees. When the fatal shot rang out, one of the men said, "Well, that'll take care of that."

After the shooting, Wallace Harvey saw a man walking briskly through the cemetery next door, holding a shotgun, headed over the ridge. He refused to say who it was. The men on the hill refused to say whose gun had fired, though they almost certainly knew. Guns made distinctive sounds, and most people could tell whose gun fired just by the sound of it.[21] But none of this was reported to the authorities. In fact, all of this was reported later, to family only, and then years later to Rick.

Several reports were made to local authorities, though. They all pointed to twenty seven year-old Bush Breazeale and his friend Ephraim "Eph" Miller. Kate Miller reported that Bush had been in her home five days before the murder, and had told her that Brack would be dead before court resumed session in eight days. Eph Miller reportedly told William Collins the same thing: Brack would be dead before court resumed. Eph offered to bet Collins, with witnesses, but Collins refused.

Others came forward with testimony about what Bush and Eph had been doing on the day of the murder. One person saw Bush in the area just before dark, holding a gun. Someone else had seen him riding away from the scene, his horse worn out. In official court documents, John Hembree said he loaded a double-barreled shotgun with rifle balls on the day of the murder and that "...this gun was placed, on loan, in the hands of the defendant." Hembree further stated for the record that "...by other witnesses, it will be shown how this was, on the same day of the killing, in the possession of the defendant..." The balls he claimed to have loaded were similar to the ones taken from Brack Smith's body. They matched Bush's bullet molds. Paper wadding used in the murder weapon had been found near Brack's body. It matched wallpaper in Bush's home.

More reports came in. Mollie Monger and Joe Harvey told authorities that they saw Eph Miller taking a double-barreled shotgun to Bush's home the evening of the murder. Mollie seemed convinced that it was the same shotgun Hembree described. Joe Harvey thought Eph Miller was hurried and anxious. Sam Miles said that when Eph came out of Bush's house, he was without the shotgun. Hulet Blackburn claimed to have seen the gun being taken from Bush's house after the killing. The most damning accusation came a few days after the shooting, when Bush ran into young Francis Smith at the store. The boy pointed to Bush and said, "He was the killer."

For a prosecutor, this was enough to seek an indictment. On December 18, 1891, four months after the shooting, Bush was indicted by a grand jury. Arrested in Kingston on January 6th, 1892, he was imprisoned there awaiting trial. The jail, since torn down, had eight rooms in the back. In the front was the Sheriff's office. Bush, accused of killing a constable, spent the next four months right behind the dead man's office. Eph Miller, also indicted, was arrested three months later, on April 15. The trial began on June 11, 1892, in Kingston.

Prosecutor M. C. Smith called fifteen witnesses for the state. Five of them had the last name Smith. John Hembree testified, as well as John Harvey and Hulet Blackburn. One of Beth's distant relatives, Charles Waller, joined them in testifying for the prosecution, as did Bush's relative Elkanah Littleton. Everyone who lived in Cave Creek was connected to the trial in some way or another. Curtis Johnston, who lived in Cave Creek when I visited that day, remembered that his grandfather's uncle was one of Bush's guards. After the Civil War and Bush's live funeral, the Brack Smith murder trial was probably the biggest event in Cave Creek history.

Court records show that no one was called to testify for the defense. Perhaps the handwritten court records I found were incomplete; they were only two pages long. But they were all I could find, and all the testimony they record, both of witnesses and the physical evidence, was lined up against Bush and Miller.

I found their acquittal astonishing.

The jury returned a verdict of "Not Guilty," on all counts. Bush and Miller were released immediately. Not only were they not punished by the court, no punishment was issued by their churches. Censure by the church was far more common than criminal conviction, but they avoided this, too. They were completely exonerated, despite what seemed like a mountain of evidence against them. Yet as I dug deeper, I realized that it was probably not the spectacular miscarriage of justice I initially thought. Rick showed me that the prosecution's case was in trouble from the start.

The April 18, 1892 Chattanooga Times article recounting Eph's arrest described the evidence against him as 'circumstantial.' No motive had been established by the prosecution. The only eyewitness was an eight year old child whose testimony could not be trusted. The physical evidence proved no direct link. Anyone could have used Bush's molds or taken part of his wallpaper in an effort to frame him. When Bush was seen riding his spent horse away from the crime scene, it turned out that it was in the opposite direction of his home. When Molly Munger saw Eph give Bush a gun that evening, it was three miles away, over the ridge, and there was no way Bush could have made it to Brack's house by the time of the killing. There were a lot of dots, but the prosecution was unable to connect them beyond a reasonable doubt. Bush had probably been innocent.

Locals, though, knew how to connect the dots of this crime. They had lived with Brack Smith for years, and no one but his family was sad to see him go. Rick told me that the one thing the prosecution could not establish, motive, was painfully obvious to anyone who lived in Cave Creek during his childhood. Though the Civil War had ended over thirty five years before, it claimed another life with the murder of Brack Smith.

I was learning that the devastation of the Civil War went far beyond lives lost. The economic scars ran deep. Valuables had been stolen. Homes and barns were burned. Large amounts of goods were confiscated by both sides. It was a war fought by guerillas and armies and both took a lasting toll not just in lives, but on the economy. I found a bill submitted by John Robinson, Beth's ancestor, who ran Robinson Mill during the war, to the United States government for $1,287. That was the value of the goods the Union army took from him in 1863. The list of items included 217 bushels of corn, eighteen acres of timber, fifty bushels of sweet potato, and twenty five gallons of molasses, at a time when most people lived off the crops they grew. Robinson was eventually reimbursed, since he had supported the Union, but he did not get the money until 1881. It took eighteen years for him to be repaid. If he had not supported the Union, or if his property had been taken by Confederates, he would have received no compensation at all.

The economic damage of the Civil War set East Tennessee back almost a hundred years. Before Bush was born, farmers in Cave Creek commonly had extra crops to sell. Along with wild picked goods, such as chestnuts and ginseng, they would be shipped upriver to Knoxville, the regional trading hub. Tennessee ginseng often ended up in China, and Chinese pottery was shipped back. Before the war, trade with the rest of the country and world flowed. After, people barely had enough to live on, and trade with the rest of the country and world decreased significantly.[22]

I had expected that most of the damage had been done during the war, but I found out that the worst years were actually after the war ended, from 1865 to 1880. All three decades after the war saw economic decline.[23] The 1880's were better, but then the economy worsened again. Despite the South having fewer people, more businesses failed there from 1889 to 1896 than in the North.[24] The economic hardships made it hard to forget the war. The recriminations hadn't helped either, as this note Steve found in the Cave Creek Missionary Baptist Church records revealed:

Aug 1865 - Whereas some of our brethren and sisters have beene engaged in bringing about the rebellion of 1861 which has brought the deth of many of our sons and oure daughters made widows and their children orphans and drenched our land and country in blud, the church declares them in disorder. Br. Henry BOGART being present and failing to make the church satisfyed and being charged with aideing and abetting in bringing on the rebellion the church excludes him for the same too. Lucindy BOGART being charged with unchristianlike conduct in aiding and abetting in said rebellion, a charge against her, she is excluded for the same. Benjamin B. CROWE and wife Mary are also charged with aiding and abetting in said rebellion. [sic]

Obviously, from the above report, many East Tennessee churches did not consider aiding the confederacy "Christian conduct." This particular church even went so far as "excluding" (the Baptist word for excommunicating) members for supporting the Confederacy. Rick Holt called it "withdrawing the hand of fellowship." Those who had supported the Confederacy were no longer allowed to be part of their church. They were actually among the lucky ones.

Daniel Foute had lived in Cades Cove, which became a popular tourist destination in Smoky Mountain National Park. Foute had been an ardent Confederate supporter during the Civil War. In 1865, he was tied up behind a horse and dragged all the way to Knoxville. Naturally, he died along the way. Foute had been killed because honor demanded it; honor was the main reason that bad blood from the Civil War lingered, and why Brack Smith was killed.[25]

As a Yankee, honor made little sense to me. Even as far back as the Civil War, Northerners were taught dignity rather than honor. Dignity is the belief that everyone has inherent value. A person with dignity can ignore an insult because they believe in self-worth regardless of what another person thinks. That was how I was raised.

The Scots-Irish who settled East Tennessee brought with them a culture of honor rather than dignity. Honor is external. It is one's standing within the community. An insult that damaged someone's honor lowered their status in the community. Therefore, it had to be addressed. Though honor was foreign to me, I came to appreciate how much simpler it is. There is little room for decision making. Insults must be addressed. Honor must be satisfied. It's just that simple. Historically, suicide rates have been higher in the North than in the South, perhaps because dignity can be questioned. Honor cannot. You either have it, or you don't, and if you don't, then you need to go get it back from the person who took it from you. Simple.[26]

Honor is the root of much of the distinctively Southern politeness. Language in the South evolved to protect honor. A person's thoughts or feelings were irrelevant. One night, Beth and her friend, Kara, laughed hilariously remembering how their friends used to say, "Y'all, we need to pray for her!" before describing in lurid detail the terrible things someone had done. It was gossip in an honorable guise. The thought or feeling behind the words were not what mattered most. What mattered was that the words were said in an honorable way. I learned through observation that as long as something was done in an honorable way, a person could get away with an awful lot.[27]

The honor system had a process for dealing with insults. When an insult was given in Bush's day, honor required an apology. If one was given, the insult would be forgiven. If not, then violence was necessary. Violent satisfaction of honor was one reason why the South was, and remains, more violent than the North. By the end of the Civil War, the South was the only place where dueling still occurred. The South has historically had the highest rates of murder, assault, death sentences, and handgun ownership in the country; honor could not be satisfied by the law. It had to be settled by a man; a woman couldn't do it, culturally. When honor was at stake, a man had to take matters into his own hands and use violence.[28] I believe that this complicated honor system is why Brack Smith was killed.

Though most of East Tennessee was pro-Union during the Civil War, the wealthy tended to support the Confederacy. There were many exceptions, of course, but generally speaking, wealthy East Tennesseans were Confederates. Brack Smith came from a wealthy family of Confederate supporters. His father, a Confederate soldier, had been murdered in Knoxville much like Daniel Foute. Smith's father was buried in a Masonic cemetery near Beth's mom's house.

Cave Creek, though, was mostly poor and pro-Union. When I visited Cave Creek Cemetery, it was dotted with gravestones that read "1st Tennessee Infantry Regiment." Formally known as the 1st Regiment Tennessee Volunteer Infantry, this was the volunteer Union regiment in which Cave Creek men served during the Civil War. Of all the Confederate states, Tennessee had the most Union soldiers. Members snuck out of Tennessee along their own underground railroad to Barbourville, Kentucky. From there they went to Camp Dick Robinson in Lancaster, Garrard County, Kentucky, where the regiment mustered. There were no Confederate gravestones in Cave Creek Cemetery, and it was easy to see that all of these men who had fought for the Union would not be happy about having a Confederate sympathizer in their midst.

Things probably would have remained peaceful if Brack Smith had been able to let the war go, but he had not. For Smith, the Civil War remained a constant source of tension and debate. He told anyone and everyone what he thought about the war, the Union, and the wrongs done to his family and others by its supporters. Smith felt that his family had not been treated honorably during or after the war. Though the rest of his family had moved on, he couldn't. This is how many notorious Southern blood feuds got started. Every time Smith spoke about the war, he dishonored the Union veterans and their families all around him. The only thing that kept Smith alive was his status as a Constable and a member of a powerful family.[29]

What pushed the matter over the edge was that Brack Smith was more than just a vocal Confederate. He was a bully who was feared and despised in Cave Creek. Locals felt that he was far too rough in how he applied his power. Court documents show that when he tried to arrest J. T. Boling in 1882, he ended up shooting him, which resulted in a charge of felonious assault. According to Rick Holt, the Smith family's powerful political connections got Brack off. One of his brothers, Frank, was a prominent professor at the University of Tennessee. His other brother, William, was a judge in Knoxville. A third brother, Mel, was a respected lawman in Cave Creek, while a fourth brother was Tennessee Commissioner of Education. They pulled strings, and Smith was acquitted.[30]

After his acquittal, Brack Smith kept his brutal ways. In early 1891, he again shot someone while making an arrest. This time it was Bill Hall, one of Bush Breazeale's good friends and neighbors. Court documents show that Hall took legal action, pressing the matter to the fullest extent of the law. Once again, Brack Smith's family came to the rescue. In August 1891 he got off a second time. This acquittal took place just before his murder. Twice Brack Smith had almost killed a respected resident of Cave Creek, and twice his wealthy, well-connected family had gotten him off. The feeling in Cave Creek was that if something wasn't done, it was only a matter of time before Brack Smith shot someone else. The next time his victim might not survive. If Smith had not been such a vocal Confederate, the community might have looked past these crimes. But they were tired of his violence and tired of him insulting their military service. Someone had to stop him.

Brack Smith's second acquittal came during a period of particularly high tension across the South. The Gilded Age of American industrialization, from 1870 to 1890, had made men like J.P. Morgan, Andrew Carnegie and John D. Rockefeller fabulously wealthy, but it had passed by East Tennessee.[31] The economic panic of 1890 did not, however, and quite a few businesses in the region were brought down. As a result, crime rose. Not just theft, either. Violent crime and homicide rates rose as well. The 1890's were the peak of mob violence in the United States, and it was most prevalent in the South. Most of these killings were matters of honor, wherein the government had failed in what was considered its primary role: protecting people and property.[32]

Southern crimes were less likely to be prosecuted than in the North, and convictions were also less frequent. Locals preferred to handle justice like they handled most things: on their own.[33] From 1885 to1903 there were 3,337 reported mob killings in the United States. Three fourths of those were in the

South. In the lowland South, violence was usually perpetrated by whites against blacks. In the mountains, like East Tennessee, the population was only ten percent black, yet there was still mob violence. It was whites killing and injuring other whites, which was called "whitecapping." Regardless of the victim's race, the 1890's saw plenty of mob violence in the South.[34] In this time of easy violence, Brack Smith pushed the community to its limit, and while he may not have been killed by a mob, his murder was covered up by one.

Brack Smith's murder is an example of what Bertram Wyatt-Brown referred to as an "expression of a family-centered community will." It was a murder that most of the community wanted. Sure, Smith's family wasn't very happy about it, but they were very much in the minority. The community wanted Smith dead for being a Confederate and a bully. They had stepped in where the courts could not. If Bush had killed Smith and it had not been sanctioned, Bush himself would have been the victim of reprisal. Besides beatings, common methods included being tarred and feathered or whipped. I believe that the fact that neither Bush nor Eph Miller were punished or even reprimanded for killing Brack Smith demonstrates it was sanctioned. It was "community justice", and so those who had killed Smith were protected.[35]

"Community justice" went beyond punishing crime. A great example is a story Rick told me about an unnamed Cave Creek man who refused to work. Rick did not know the reason he didn't work; maybe the man was a drunk, or maybe he was just lazy. Regardless, the man had a family, and if he did not work, his family went hungry. However, not working is not a crime. The local authorities could not do anything, but the community could. So, one night a group of men left a pile of switches on his porch as a warning. (Switches are thin, supple sticks used for whipping.) The guy did not take the hint, so the next night, they dragged him out of his house and whipped him with those switches in his own backyard. Early the next morning he was out in the field working. From that point on, he did his duty and provided for his family.

Even if the killing of Brack Smith had not been tacitly sanctioned, there was a good chance Bush and Eph Miller would have been acquitted. Alexis de Tocqueville, the famous French philosopher, once spoke with a young lawyer in Alabama about criminals going unpunished in the South.

"But when a man is killed like that," asked de Tocqueville, "is his assassin not punished?"

"He is always brought to trial," answered the lawyer, "and always acquitted by jury, unless there are greatly aggravating circumstances…This violence has become accepted. Each juror feels that he might, on leaving the court, find himself in the same position as the accused, and he acquits."[36]

There were many methods of securing an acquittal. Judges dismissed on technicalities. Juries found defendants not guilty despite overwhelming evidence. Sometimes, the accused would simply vanish from custody and reappear at home, as if nothing had ever happened. In Bush's case, the trial proceeded, but it was sabotaged in many ways. Some witnesses simply failed to show up when they were due to testify. Others stalled long enough that the government gave up on ever speaking to them. The official reports were disconnected and failed to hold up under scrutiny. The very fact that Bush and Miller were so quickly identified was surprising and suspicious. I believe that the people of Cave Creek successfully deflected attention away from the real killers, but did so in a way that would ensure that Bush and Miller never got convicted. It worked.

Unfortunately, though, some things never change. Then, as now, innocent until proven guilty only exists in the court of law. Though a few locals knew who was truly guilty, the rest did not. In the absence of someone else to blame, many believed Bush was the killer. To those without intimate knowledge of Cave Creek, it seemed like a cold blooded murder. Bush's reputation in the wider community was tarnished. He became the Boogeyman of Cave Creek.

Chapter Three

The Boogeyman of Cave Creek

Uncle Bush Breazeale was only twenty-seven years old when he was acquitted of the murder of Brack Smith. Found innocent, he should have gone home, met a nice girl, had a bunch of kids, a gaggle of grandkids, and lived happily ever after. That seemed to me to be the way it was supposed to work.

That was not what happened.

I found that out when I finally met someone who had known Bush well. That meeting came about in a very East Tennessee way: a chance encounter over lunch. Bush's live funeral was put on by Beth's great-grandfather, Frank Quinn, who had owned Quinn Funeral Home in Loudon. The home had changed its name to McGill-Karnes, but had been operating continuously ever since. Through the years, we had gotten to know one of the owners, Renee McGill. She had long brown hair and a warm smile. We shared a taste for barbecue, and when Beth and I went to Calhoun's Restaurant's barbecue lunch buffet one day, we saw Renee there. As she always did when we saw her, Renee asked if there was anything new with the movie. Then she asked me to come speak to the Loudon Rotary Club. About twenty business and community leaders would gather to hear me. Renee gave me the date and time, and I told her I would be there.

Once again I stayed at Beth's mom's house. Shortly before I was supposed to leave, I looked at Beth, thoughtful.

"What?" she asked. She probably expected me to ask her what to wear. That was something I always struggled with in Loudon, where the attire was more conservative than Atlanta. Actually, I struggled with it in Atlanta, too, I just struggled more in Loudon.

"I don't think they ever told me where to meet," I said.

"Why would they?" she asked. "Everyone knows where they meet."

"Just drive around," Beth's mom suggested. "You'll see 'em."

Right.

I called Renee, and Beth's Uncle Dave, who lived in Loudon. Neither of them picked up. Next was Uncle Bill, who answered, but he didn't know either. Apparently everyone didn't know where the Rotary Club met. Bill said he would make a couple of phone calls, and I set off in the car, hoping someone would figure it out. During my twenty-minute drive to Loudon Bill, Dave, and Renee all called me back to tell me that the meeting was at the annex basement of the First Baptist Church.

Did any of them offer to tell me where that was?

Of course not, but this time I knew enough to ask.

Fortunately, it was very easy to find. I drove west across the tall bridge over the Tennessee River into

Loudon, and through the first light. The church was one hundred feet down, on the right. Brick with four white columns, it had wide stairs along the length of the front. The Baptist Church Annex was around the back. In Loudon, there are many things that start with 'the'. There was The Methodist Church, The Baptist Church, The Parade, The Ice Cream Shop. The Baptist Church Annex was where Beth's parents had their wedding reception, even though they were married at The Methodist Church.

In the bright white basement of the annex, a buffet lunch had been set up. Twenty Rotary members were already eating around a "U" of eight long tables. Renee and I each had salad, chicken fingers, ham, green beans (with bacon in them), a biscuit and sweet tea. While we were eating, she pointed to a short, older gentleman in the back. He wore an open collared white shirt with black checks, glasses, and pressed black slacks. He was thin, his short hair neatly trimmed.

"That's J.Y. McNabb," Renee told me. "You need to talk to him. He was at Bush's funeral. And if you let him get away from you now, you'll never get him back." Even though he looked too young, only seventy or so, I made sure to meet J.Y. after the speech.

It turned out that J.Y. McNabb was actually in his mid-eighties. During World War II, he left his rural home and joined the army. He landed, along with the Fourth Armored Division, in the first wave on the beaches of Normandy on D-Day. I later discovered that, according to most historians, the Fourth Armored Division landed a month after D-Day. If you want to tell a man that he's wrong about when and where people were shooting at him, have at it. I took him at his word.

"You were in the first wave at Normandy?" I repeated when J.Y. mentioned it. I had not expected to be talking to a hero.

"Yeah," he said, looking a little embarrassed. "Yeah."

"Wow."

"Yeah. We lost a lot of boys over there, boy I'll tell you," he said. "When that green light come on in that little ol' boat they had us on, boy you had to hit it, you know? Some of them drowned there. The British pilots, they didn't want to go too close in; they'd give the green light, and a lot of them got drowned."

I didn't know what to say. I just listened.

J.Y fought across France. Most famously, he fought under General George Patton in the Battle of the Bulge. Through all of his service, eventually fighting his way all the way into Germany, he "only got shot one time." J.Y. was not embarrassed to tell me it was right through both sides of both cheeks of his rear end. He had refused to be evacuated because then he would never have been reunited with his unit. So he had fought through it, even though he hadn't been able to sit down for a while.

Eventually, we got to talking about Bush. J.Y. also grew up in Cave Creek. World Wars I and II took young men like him all over the world, while some of his relatives never went further than twenty miles. Rick Holt had spoken with a woman who had lived three miles over the ridge from Cave Creek, but had never been there. J.Y. McNabb fought his way around the globe, went back to his rural home, and never left again.

I was surprised to learn from J.Y. that Bush had actually lived in Dogwood, a loose collection of a dozen farmsteads just over the western ridge of Cave Creek. It was close enough that Bush was good friends with J.Y.'s dad, Sam McNabb. Sam had been mentioned several times in the newspaper articles I had read. When J.Y. was young, Bush would come visit Sam. The two men would sit on the porch and talk. Bush often stayed for an hour, and many times it was longer than that. When J.Y. and I met, the visiting tradition was still a part of life in East Tennessee. The main difference is that now, people usually, but don't always, call first. Bush would not have called, because neither he nor Sam had a phone. Instead, Bush would just stop by and they would visit. He spent a lot of time on Sam McNabb's porch, and J.Y. spent a lot of time listening to them talk.

"Best thing I knew about Bush was that he was a guy that didn't talk too much," J.Y. said. "I thought he was a good guy, but you know, they had it out on him that he had shot somebody. I don't think that really happened. I don't know. I was more or less listening then."

It was J.Y. who first gave me insight into what life was like for Bush after he was acquitted for the murder of Brack Smith. While J.Y. and his father liked Bush, he told me that most of their community did not. Bush was an old man then, and a pariah. People were scared of him. They would say terrible things, like "Bush Breazeale is coming! You better get your kids in the house." When he would ride his mule down the road, people would get out of the way. Many avoided him altogether. Bush had become the Boogeyman.

Bush's reputation only got worse as he got older. The past had a habit of sticking with folks in East Tennessee. It still does. One example is the prevalence and durability of nicknames. Most of the men that I have met in East Tennessee, and more than a few women, had one.

Beth's uncle, Tree, once went on a trip with eleven other Loudon men to play golf in North Augusta, South Carolina. A reporter for one of the local TV stations in nearby Augusta, Georgia (home of the Masters Golf Tournament) came by to interview golfers about heart attacks on the golf course. She happened across a foursome of Loudon residents: Henry Julian, Mayor of Loudon Bernie Swiney, Charles White and Doug Montooth. Mayor Swiney proceeded to tell her all about having not one but two heart attacks on a golf course. After the camera was turned off, she asked everyone's name, for the story. She was told by the storyteller, Mayor Swiney, that his name was Inky. His playing partners that day were Jam Up, Skip and Huggy Bear. The reporter interrupted to ask if anyone had a regular name. She was told no, and that the others on the trip were Tree, Flop, Floppy, Frog, Buck, Dickie, Chuck, and Ed.

Those nicknames were mild by Loudon standards. Devil Catcher Henderson and Bad Eye Wallace were two of my favorites. Cowhide Christian was another good one. His son was Calf Hide Christian. There were two men nicknamed Dough Belly: Dough Belly Dobson and Dough Belly Brown. I never did find anyone who remembered Dough Belly Brown's real first name.[37]

As I said, these monikers show how the past tends to stick to a person in East Tennessee. White Store got his nickname because he managed the White Store. Beth's great aunt, Eleanor Barnes, was called Pete her whole life because as a child her personality resembled Wild West hero Pistol Pete. Beth's Uncle Dave, her father's brother, was 'Tree' because he was so tall. Once a nickname stuck, it never went away.

Bush's nickname had an innocuous origin. It was short for Bushaloo, his middle name, which was a family name stretching back generations. No one I met knew why he was called Uncle, though. Neither nickname was bad, especially when compared with Bad Eye or Devil Catcher, but the cultural memory of Bush's alleged complicity in Brack Smith's murder lingered nonetheless. Even though the specific accusations against him were slowly forgotten in the years after the trial, Bush's reputation grew worse. In the years before his live funeral, even distant family members had come to look down on him.

I learned that through Beth's Uncle Bill, who lived just outside Loudon on Littleton Road, which was named for Bush's mother's family. Before he retired, Bill worked with Don Breazeale, a very distant relative of Bush. Don was tall, thin, and in his mid-fifties, with white hair and glasses. He spoke with a deep baritone. Don lived on Breazeale Road, thought it had only recently been given that name. When a 911 system was installed, the road required a name. Since it was on the original Breazeale farmstead, Breazeale Road it became.

Right next to Don's home was the foundation of an old Breazeale farmhouse. It sat in a pasture valley. Across the street, at the edge of one of the fields, lay the old Breazeale Cemetery. Don's close relatives and Bush's distant ones were buried there; there were sixteen Breazeales interred, along with three Prices, two Blackburns, and one baby, whose grave read simply "Thomas E." There were no other houses in sight. The closest one, around the bend, belonged to Don's elderly parents. Don took me to meet them, and I learned that even Bush's own relations looked down on him.

Neither of Don's parents had attended Bush's live funeral. Don's dad hadn't gone because his mother had refused to give him permission.

"His mother didn't want to claim kin to Bush," Don's mother told me as we sat on reclining chairs in the living room of their ranch home, where the only sounds of civilization were our voices.

"When it was brought up to my grandmother," Don added, "the subject was quickly changed."

"What really made my mother mad," Don's father chimed in with a baritone just like his son's, "was that when I was in high school, some of them around here hung 'Bush Breazeale' on me." That meant that they had tried to make "Bush" his nickname. His mother knew how nicknames stuck and would have none of that. Don's grandmother, it turned out, came from the Smith family.

"The Smiths was a moneyed family, from Roane County," Don's father continued. "They owned the whole area down in there. They were just proud, she was just a proud woman. She was used to that, she was looked up to. The family was looked up to-"

"She just looked down on Bush," Don's mother chimed in. "They said he kept his horse in the house with him."

"He kept his mule in one part of the house, and he lived in another," added Don's dad.

"But your mother was a Smith," I interrupted. "I wonder if she was related to the fellow Bush was rumored to have shot."

"I doubt that very seriously," Don's mother said. "There are a lot of Smiths in this area. Everywhere you go there are Smiths." Obviously, that was true, as it would be anywhere in America, but I was learning that family connections ran deep in East Tennessee, and they were connected to social class.

Classism in East Tennessee was rooted in the culture of the Scots-Irish settlers, and did not seem to have changed much over time. Nor did it seem unique. It seems like every place I've lived, every history book I've read, and every culture I've studied has people who are "in" and people who are "out." East Tennessee was no different, but the distinctions between the two seemed more pronounced there. People seemed more eager to classify others than they had been where I grew up.

Mimi and Granddaddy, for instance, were respected. One reason for their respectability was their behavior. They did not swear, nor drink. Nor did they wear clothes out in public that showed any skin other than hands and faces. Granddaddy only wore short sleeves to mow the lawn. Beth never once saw him in actual shorts. Neither could she remember seeing Uncle Steve or Uncle Larry in shorts. A short-sleeved shirt with long pants was as casual as they got. Shorts were out of the question for them, no matter the heat or humidity.

Like many styles of dress, this sense of fashion was born out of practical necessity. Hats, long sleeves and long pants were initially preferred because they provided shelter from the elements. Practicality created fashion, and being covered up became a sign of modesty and propriety. A respectable person would rather suffer severe heat, even passing out, than the indignation of being improperly dressed no matter the occasion.

I was surprised to learn that proper attire varied with income. Whereas Mimi and Granddaddy wore suits to church on Sunday, Bush had no suit. Yet everyone was expected to wear their "Sunday best."

Many people had only one suit, especially in the 1930s and 40s, but they wore that one suit to church every week.[38] Whatever someone's best was, they were expected to wear it. Bush probably had a couple of pairs of pants, a couple of shirts, a jacket, and a hat. Maybe some socks. That was it. But if he wore the best he had to church, then that was respectable. More than how much someone had, it was the choices people made that determined their respectability. Bush, by all accounts, dressed properly, but there were other factors in determining respectability. These were where Bush failed to meet the standards of the community.

After Get Low came out, Knoxville television stations ran stories related to the real Uncle Bush. WBIR-11 reporter Lee Ann Bowman did an interview that aired on August 27, 2010, with John Harvey Smith, grandson of Brack Smith. In his late eighties, John Harvey burned with a hatred for Bush that had been given new fuel by the movie. After I saw the interview, I wanted to hear more from John Harvey. I called Rick Holt, hoping that Rick could convince John Harvey to speak with me. When Rick called to set up an interview, John Harvey was downright rude, but you would only know that if you knew how to read between the lines.

"Who do you want to bring over with you?" John Harvey asked.

"One of the writers of 'Get Low'," Rick told him.

"You mean 'Get Low' down," John Harvey said.

"I'm sorry, what?" Rick was shocked.

"You mean Get Low down," John Harvey repeated.

For me, adding "down" at the end had no meaning. It sounded like a dance move. Rick, though, understood that it was a pretty nasty thing to say. Mimi, Granddaddy, and anyone wanting to be respectable would never have used actual swear words. Honor did not allow it. "Low down" was about as strong a put-down as a respectable person would ever use. It was a polite way of saying something was filthy and despicable. John Harvey Smith thought that the movie was awful, and he stated his reason very clearly, and respectably, to Rick in that WBIR interview.

"I don't know why he should be shown any respect," John Harvey said about Bush in the television interview. If John Harvey had bothered to see "Get Low," or to meet me, then he would have learned that the movie does not glorify the character of Bush. Writing a movie about someone does not mean they are being lifted up as a role model. But John Harvey had his mind made up about our movie, and he had his mind made up about Bush Breazeale, and like his ancestor, Brack Smith, he let everybody know it.

"He was considered a murderer, a thief, and a moonshiner," John Harvey said on television. John Harvey was raised on the same property that Rick Holt was, only years earlier. It was the same property on which his grandfather had been murdered. "I didn't know (Bush) that well. I'd just see him occasionally pass by the house, but I didn't know him personally. I never did have any fear of him, but other people did, I've been told. They said they got the children out of the yard when Bush came down the road."

That was the first I had heard of Bush being a thief or a moonshiner. Although, despite these allegations, what surprised me the most was that John Harvey was the only other person I'd met who had mentioned Brack Smith. Other than Rick and him, no one else I had met knew about the murder. Brack Smith seemed to have been forgotten, along with the details of the murder charges against Bush. By the time J.Y. McNabb was a boy, there was just a rumor that he had shot someone, that there may have been a murder. Plenty of other rumors had popped up, though, as John Harvey had mentioned. Nothing was ever proven, but when some trinket went missing, Bush was blamed. Children were pulled off the street when he rode by. Bush's reputation was destroyed by these rumors of dishonorable behavior, and he dropped to the bottom rung of the social ladder.

But were the rumors true? Was Bush really a thief? Was he a moonshiner? J.Y. McNabb and his father had thought Bush was a decent fellow. Granddaddy had never said anything that would make me, or Beth, think Bush had been trouble. I was getting mixed signals, and it was confusing. I decided to start looking in a different direction. I stopped asking people what they thought of Bush and started investigating the man himself.

Chapter Four

Uncle Bush

At the time of his trial, Bush was already considered an old bachelor. Newspaper articles said that Bush had never married. When asked by the Knoxville Journal why he had never married, Bush was quoted as saying "I never did happen upon anyone I wanted to marry, except those I couldn't git. Them I could git the devil wouldn't have."[39] I never found anyone who could tell me who Bush could have gotten or who he had wanted. What was clear, though, was that he never married, and lived alone at the time of his funeral. In fact, he spent almost his entire life living in one house. The only time he lodged any-

Wilson, Delmont. "Back Home After His Funeral." June 27, 1938.
Knoxville News Sentinel, Knoxville, TN.

where else was when he was in jail, and once on a "round-trip to Missouri in an ox wagon when [he] was eight years old."[40] I hoped that a visit to Bush's home would tell me who he really was.

Newspaper articles said that Bush lived on Dogwood Road, but I couldn't find that on any online map. Not only did Dogwood Road not exist, the odds were it never had. When it was built, Dogwood Road was probably the only road in town. Why would it need a name? Besides, an address was not needed to find a house in Dogwood when Bush lived there. It was twelve scattered farmsteads and a church. If you wanted to find someone, all you had to do was knock on a few doors and ask. It was actually considered normal to stop and ask a neighbor where someone lived. They would probably try to connect you to someone they knew, to make sure you were respectable. If you were, they would be happy to tell you where to find whoever you sought.

Rather than knocking on strangers' doors, I called Rick Holt and asked him if he would help me find Bush's home. He just laughed. He already knew where Bush's house was.

"Everyone in Cave Creek knows that!" he said.

Duh.

I took another trip to Tennessee, and Rick, Steve and I hopped in a car and drove over. To get to Dogwood, we had to drive through Cave Creek. We drove along the valley bottom on Cave Creek Road, with the stream on our right and forested ridges above us on both sides. The road bent where it neared the Tennessee River; this was where the ferry and store had been. We followed the two-lane road to the right, up the ridge, and came down in the next valley over. That was Dogwood Valley, where Bush had lived.

Our first left was Little Dogwood Valley Road. We turned there. It was aptly named. Unlike Cave Creek Road, it lacked center lines and shoulders. My stomach got queasy just looking at it. As we made the turn, we could see Dogwood School ahead. Built in 1892 and abandoned in 1960, this one room schoolhouse was tightly surrounded by trees. A few of them in the narrow patch of earth between the school and the road were almost a food in diameter. The reddish hue of the faded brown clapboard exterior was all that remained of the school's original color. I asked

Dogwood School - Author's collection, 2010

Steve and Rick if they minded if we stopped and took a look. They didn't, so we pulled over and got out.

Twenty-five feet wide and forty feet long, the school had three large, evenly spaced windows on the long walls. Oddly, it was two stories tall but had only one floor, which meant that the only room had a ceiling twice normal height. The blackboard was a black rectangle painted on the end wall. A hanging chimney once attached to a wood burning stove in the middle of the far wall, but it had fallen down. On the wall near where the chimney stood, names had been written. One was S.A. Littleton, possibly a relative of Bush's mother, Sarah Jane Littleton.

We got back in the car to see where Sarah and her husband had raised their family. We were now on Wolf Creek Road, which was one lane. At least it was paved. As we wound around several corners, we passed a couple of isolated homes. When we came to a Y intersection, Cate Road veered off to the left. We took it because this one-lane dirt road was where Bush had lived, in the second house on the left. Its owner lived in the first, a double-wide trailer above a cinder block basement, set a hundred feet off the road. Rick suggested we pay him a visit before we went to look at Bush's house.

"Let me go talk to him," Rick said. "Folks around here don't like outsiders much."

No kidding.

Ironically, the man who owned Bush's house was from Pennsylvania. He still wasn't keen on outsiders, though. Butch Van Voris was his name, and his pure white Van Dyke beard made him look older than his fifty-five years. In 1988, Butch had bought the property at auction because he wanted to "live away from people." He got his wish. With the exception of the two houses, there was nothing in sight but nature. I couldn't even hear any cars passing. In that sense, Bush's farmstead had changed little. A newspaper article published the day of his live funeral described his cabin:

> "No radio or telephone is in the Breazeale home. The faint sound of automobile horns on the highway five miles away and the occasional drone of an airplane motor furnish the only evidence to make a person aware of the outside world."[41]

Bush's cabin felt that way the day of our visit. In terms of its isolation and closeness to nature, it had not changed a bit in seventy years. In the twenty years Butch had owned Bush's cabin, the three of us were the first people to come to look at it.

"The house is so remote," he said, "that most people think it's lost, even though it's never been hidden."

Butch pointed, and I turned to look. The two houses were close enough that Butch was using Bush's cabin as a storage shed. Slightly downhill was the home where Bush was born, and where he lived for virtually his whole life. Like many farm homes of the time, Bush's was built on a north facing slope to shelter it from wind and storms.[42] We were behind it, so we walked down the slight grade and around to the front. Only four steps, a low wall, and a short

Butch Van Voris (left) and Uncle Steve outside Bush's cabin
Author's collection, 2010

walkway separated Bush's home from the road. It was a white, two-story house with clapboard siding and a full- length front porch. The exterior siding was modern in appearance, wood just like I had on my house, though the white paint on Bush's home was in much worse shape.

Only the roof gave away the building's age. For one, it was made of shake, two inch thick pieces of oak chopped into rough squares and used as shingles. Also, the shape of the roof revealed that there had been several additions. The steepest parts of the roof were original. Each successive addition had a shallower slope, a clear indication that they were added later. If it had all been built at once, the roof would have had a single slope.

This was where Bush was born on June 29, 1864, the seventh of nine children. Six to eight children was average, though fifteen was not unusual. Like most homes of the time, bathroom facilities were an out-house located down a short trail out the back, near the edge of the field. Heat and cooking were done with wood stoves. There was no running water or electricity.[43] Despite the fact that he had come here to get away from people, Butch was happy to give us a tour.

There were four sections to the interior of Bush's house. In the front was a covered porch, which had been added by later owners. Front porches were common during Bush's life; a transition between the home and the elements, they were where visitors were met and entertained. Porches weren't inside, they weren't outside, but rather they were in the middle. Today that place is Starbucks. If a modern American wants to talk with someone in a casual, comfortable place that feels like home but isn't quite that intimate, they meet at Starbucks. As that role was filled by front porches, and visiting was so important, every older home I had seen in East Tennessee had one.

The front door opened into another addition, this one built on the floor of the original front porch. It had been turned into a living room, with a sitting room to the right. Doors led into a third section. This was the original house. Here was a relatively modern kitchen and another sitting room. Finally, an enclosed porch had been tacked onto the back. Every room was piled knee deep with all kinds of junk, only passable through narrow walking lanes. Little of the original interior remained. The walls had all been painted or paneled over, while the floors had been covered or tiled. Only the ceiling was original. It was a "tongue in groove" wooden plank ceiling. Butch said he had tried to remove it.

"I had to stop," he said. "It was too well made. You can't tear one part out without taking the whole thing down."

Pictures from the time showed that when Bush had his funeral, only the center section stood, with a small, rickety front porch. These two rooms, along with bedrooms upstairs, were the extent of the house when Bush lived in it. When the home was expanded, the two exterior front windows had been turned into interior doorways, and the original front had been made into an interior wall. It was the kind of country house that home renovators dream about restoring for an article in "Southern Living" magazine, but all of these expansions had taken place after Bush had died.

I had expected the cabin to be built of logs, but it had been framed with studs just like a modern house. Rick said this had been done in East Tennessee since the 1820's. Bush's home was not just typical of antebellum East Tennessee, it was typical of America. So were Dogwood and Cave Creek. According to one historian, "rutted and muddy highways, widely scattered villages, and homes separated by miles of wilderness characterized the majority of American farm communities until well into the twentieth century."[44] When Bush was born, his cabin had been a relatively modern home. When he died, it was a small, poor, country shack, even though the house itself had not changed. The cause was, once again, the economic devastation of the Civil War. Though it had set back the economy of the whole region, it was rural farmers who had suffered the most.

Loudon, for instance, did much better after the war than Dogwood or Cave Creek did. The population of Loudon in 1841 had been only thirty two white males over the age of twenty one. (This was the only group that was counted in the census as they were the only ones who could vote.) The town began growing in 1851, with the arrival of the East Tennessee and Georgia Railroad; Loudon became a regional transportation hub. A hotel was constructed, and over a hundred guests per week stayed there, from distant places such as Baltimore, Washington D.C., St. Louis, Boston and Cincinnati.[45] Loudon grew tremendously before the war, and continued growing after.

Farming in East Tennessee declined significantly in the decades after the war. Tennessee had led the nation in hog production in 1850, but by 1930 production had declined by sixty one percent. The more productive farms of the Midwest became the breadbasket of the country.[46] Meanwhile, businesses in Loudon grew and did well. The August 2, 1876 edition of the Loudon Times had advertisements for Italian marble, sewing machines, and various "spring and summer goods" from New York. The July 3, 1890 edition also had ads for goods from all over the country. For sale were cotton scales from Binghamton, NY, and sewing machines from Dallas and St. Louis. Plants from a nursery in Louisville, Kentucky were also available.

Loudon grew twenty five percent between 1890 and 1910,[47] while Dogwood and Cave Creek stagnated.

This was partly due to a shift in population taking place throughout Appalachia. Between 1850 and 1930, the population of urban Appalachia quadrupled. The non-farming population doubled.[48] As economic growth concentrated, a new form of classism divided the population. As people in cities and towns became wealthier than their rural brethren, they began to look down on them. Rural farmers, meanwhile, started to consider city people arrogant. The lower standard of living in rural areas did not alter this opinion one bit.[49]

Another reason behind this new classism was education. Low quality education was a regional problem in farm communities like Cave Creek and Dogwood. Before, during, and after the Civil War, education in the South lagged behind the rest of the country. In 1852, less than twenty five percent of school age children attended school in Kentucky, Georgia, Virginia and South Carolina. By contrast, in 1830, both New York and Massachusetts had school attendance rates of around seventy five percent. The typical Southern school calendar was only eighty days, half that of those in the North. The education itself was also of lower quality. Going to school seemed unproductive to many farmers, given its limited use in their daily lives.[50] According to the United States Census Bureau, illiteracy in Tennessee in 1900 was twice the national rate; one in five adults there could not read, while nationally it was only one in ten.[51] Bush himself had learned how to read, but not write. This was yet another social strike against him.

Just as people in the cities and towns of East Tennessee started looking down on people like Bush, so did the nation. In the 1800's Tennessee had produced elected Presidents Andrew Jackson and James Polk. A third President, Andrew Johnson, had served as Abraham Lincoln's Vice President and become President upon his assassination. That brief spurt meant that Tennessee was the state with the seventh highest number of Presidents, but none came after 1900. National heroes such as Davy Crockett and Sam Houston came from Tennessee, but by 1900, that well had also run dry. Tennessee failed to keep pace with the rest of the country economically, culturally and intellectually.

This caused an interesting shift in the national perception of East Tennessee. By the late 1800's, romantic images of Appalachian mountain people began appearing in popular literature. Though places like Loudon kept economic and social pace, a new wave of Southern writers emerged around 1870 and focused on the Appalachian farmer. Northerners began to fall in love with stories of these people, who were "pure, uncorrupted, 100 percent America, picturesque and photogenic premoderns who were an untapped national treasure." An example is Uncle Remus: His Songs and Sayings, by Joel Chandler Harris, a collection best known for the characters of narrator Uncle Remus and trickster Br'er Rabbit. Though not specifically Appalachian, these books and others like them introduced those outside the South to a dialect and culture that they had not known to be different.[52]

While some appreciated the distinctive culture revealed in these books, others concluded that Southerners were "backward, unhealthy, unchurched, ignorant, violent, and morally degenerate social misfits who were a national liability."[53] Regardless of how the reader viewed the characters, the immense popularity of Southern books at the beginning of the twentieth century helped cement the image of Southerners in popular culture as poor, ignorant hillbillies. Whether that image was noble or savage depended upon the reader, but it left Bush marginalized by people both inside and outside of his own community, despite the fact that Bush's life had hardly changed at all.[54]

Frank Anderson, a distant relative of Bush, told me that Bush was typical of most folks in his community, in that he "spent his life looking at the south end of a northbound mule." Bush grew up and lived in poverty, but he saw wealth when he visited Loudon and other towns nearby. Yet I found nothing to indicate that he had been a thief. There was wealth around, but no links to any actual thefts, or any other crime that would suggest to me he was a scoundrel. But had he been a moonshiner? Was John Harvey's final attack on his respectability true?

My journey towards answering that question began at Bush's house. Rick told me that in the years after his acquittal, Bush had a group of friends called "The Ridgerunners." There were four or five of them, and they went fox hunting together. The newspapers had mentioned several times that Bush was a fox hunter. After we got back from the cabin, I decided to find out more about fox hunting so I could get to know Bush better. I was feeling lazy that night, so I googled "fox hunting East Tennessee." I clicked on the first link. It opened a green and white website with a large picture of fox hunters. The words "Welcome to the Tennessee Valley Hunt" flashed up on my screen. Perfect! I poked around and found out that it was exactly what it sounded like: a fox hunting club based around Knoxville. Even better, it was an active group. Their next event was in two weeks.

From their website, I learned that the Tennessee Valley Hunt used something called the English Tradition. Hunts were genteel, regal affairs. Whole families gathered in their Sunday best. It was a festive gathering, a social event. Hunters wore the stereotypical black riding caps and solid red or black riding coats with tight black breeches and tall, shiny boots. The horses were carefully groomed, their manes sometimes braided. The hunt was led by bloodhounds who tracked the fox, the riders following behind. Foxes do not leave their home territory of approximately five square miles, so the chases were seldom in a single direction. The fox would make many twists and turns as it tried to lose its pursuers without leaving its territory.

I was surprised to find that at the end of the hunt, the fox was not killed. Instead, the goal was to get the fox to "go to ground," meaning that it was chased until it ran into a den. The hunt was then over. It was the first kind of hunting I had ever heard of that was actually hunting and not killing. The foxes were probably terrified, but at least they get to live to eat rabbits and squirrels another day. All in all, it sounded pretty interesting. I was excited, and I started telling Beth about it. We were both sitting on the couch, and she was watching TV while I read details off my laptop.

"This is so cool!" I told her.

"Uh huh," she nodded, her eyes never leaving the television screen.

"And it just came up right away, first time I searched." I was still bubbling.

"Cool," she said, without enthusiasm.

"Well, I certainly think it is."

Then she turned to me, and gave me a look. It's a look I've seen many times before. In this case, it meant "Do you really think Bush did that?" She had a point. Such a regal affair sounded too genteel for a rugged mountain man like Uncle Bush.

Which, of course, it was.

I contacted Carla Hawkinson, head of the Tennessee Valley Hunt, to see if she could tell me about the kind of fox hunting Bush might have done. Carla worked as the Equestrian Director at Blackberry Farm in Walland, TN. Nestled in the foothills of the Smoky Mountains, Blackberry Farm was a 4,200 acre luxury estate an hour east of where Bush lived. Carla said Blackberry Farm had grown from a six-bedroom inn to multiple buildings with a total of sixty-two guest rooms, including private cottages. It was a working farm with livestock, fresh produce, and a farm store, as well as some of the most expensive accommodations in the South. Blackberry Farm was exclusive, but it did provide outsiders with an authentic experience of East Tennessee's food and culture.[55] Beth's mom had stayed there once. She thought it was beautiful, but was unimpressed by the food. It was good, but no better than what Mimi had made.

Carla told me, and Rick later confirmed, that Bush's kind of fox hunting was not the kind done by the Tennessee Valley Hunt. His version was known regionally as "night hunting", though a few did call it fox hunting. When Bush was alive, lots of East Tennessee mountain men did it. Night hunters typically owned between three and five hounds. When the dogs weren't hunting, they provided defense against predators. Rabbits and groundhogs stayed out of the fields and crops when dogs were on patrol. For this reason, farm families often had several dogs.[56]

Bush and The Ridgerunners hunted deer, raccoon, and other critters up along the ridge that separated Cave Creek and Dogwood. There was a rough baseball field up there, surrounded by forest. Baseball had arrived with the Union troops during the Civil War. By 1890, it was popular even in rural areas like Cave Creek.[57] No one used the baseball field at night, so it was the Ridgerunners' private sanctuary. The other Ridgerunners were married men. Like Bush, they worked very long hours on the farm. They also had families, though, and the pressures of family, church and society were strong. They had nowhere to go where they could just be guys. Today, men can do that in their man caves or at sports bars, watching football or NASCAR or the NCAA basketball tournament on a big screen TV while drinking beer and farting. Back then, there was no socially acceptable place for men to be their manly selves. So they went night hunting.

Sometimes the Ridgerunners would take their dogs on legitimate hunts and bring back wild game to be eaten. Other times, though, they had contests. They would bring their hounds to the baseball field in the mountains at dusk and build a fire. When it was dark, they would release the hounds. The hounds would run off and find a fox, which they would chase all around the woods. Fox hounds bark as they hunt, and the hunters could easily recognize their hounds by their voices. They could also tell by the sounds the dogs made what kind of animal they were chasing, and even the exact stage of the chase. A bad hound would get distracted and go chase a deer or a raccoon. A good hound would stay on the trail until the fox went to ground. Then it would give a distinctive bark. Every time a hound got a fox to go to ground, its owner got bragging rights. That was how the Ridgerunners often went night hunting.

And while all this was going on, they got smashed on moonshine.

So during a typical night hunt, maybe the hounds would get a fox or two to go to ground. If one did, that was a bonus. If not, no big deal. It was the equivalent of guys getting together to watch a football game. If your team wins, it's great, but really the point is just to get together and have fun. That's what the Ridgerunners were doing. They were getting together to have fun and just be guys, and fox hunting was the excuse.

Naturally, I had to try it.

Unfortunately, night hunting seemed to be dead in East Tennessee. Neither Rick nor Carla knew of anyone who still did it. Rick used to know some guys who went, but they were dead. I called just about everyone I could think of, and not only was there no one to take me, I couldn't even find anyone who had done it.

Then, one day, I was in the car with Uncle Bill. We were talking about my research, and I casually mentioned that I was looking for someone who could tell me about night hunting.

"I've done it," Bill said nonchalantly.

I should have known.

But even Uncle Bill couldn't get a night lined up. I'm sure somebody up in the mountains still did some form of night hunting, but I couldn't find them. Bill did tell me that his experience of night hunting was exactly what the Ridgerunners had done; he had been part of a group of men getting smashed on moonshine while occasionally listening for their hounds barking in the night. It sounded like fun times, but I was out of luck. I was stuck with my man cave and big screen TV. Bummer.

Still, this taught me something important about Bush. If these guys liked him enough to spend their limited guy time with him, he couldn't have been that bad a person. I suppose even the worst people have friends, but not for decades. Plus, the Ridgerunners did sometimes actually hunt, so they would have been around Bush when he had a loaded gun. It seemed likely to me that they trusted him. And night hunting seemed like a fairly harmless activity. Other than the livers of the Ridgerunners, nothing and nobody got hurt. Even the foxes survived. It sounded like a normal, harmless thing for a guy to do. If this was the moonshining Bush did, then I couldn't fault him for doing it. He didn't seem like the scoundrel John Harvey had described. Not at all.

Picture appears courtesy Frank Huggins, grandson of Augustus Summers

Bush and mule - Huggins. Date unknown

Now that I had explored the rumors about Bush, his home and his hobby, I wanted to find out about his closest companion. Most farmers have livestock, and lots of people have pets. Bush's mule was both, and much more. Eighteen-years old at the time of the live funeral, the mule's name was "Mule". She was Bush's coworker, friend, and constant companion. When Bush wasn't in the house, and occasionally when he was, they spent all their time together. I once again called Carla Hawkinson, head of the Tennessee Valley Hunt, and asked her to tell me about mules. Carla's job at Blackberry farm was to help guests enjoy horseback riding in this pristine setting, and she was an expert on mules as well.

It turned out that Bush's relationship with Mule said a lot about his personality. According to Carla, while most of the plowing in the area was done by horses, the mule was by far the better plow animal. Tougher, stronger, longer-lived and more resilient, mules were better workers. The problem was that they were tougher to work with. Horses could be intimidated; if you threatened a horse with a whip, it would likely do what you wanted. Mules, on the other hand, would just dig their hooves in deeper. Carla told me that the phrase 'stubborn as a mule' was apt. Mules had more personality than horses, but just like with people, that could be good and bad. A mule had to be enticed to do what you wanted, and would do nothing to please you unless you got their respect. Once you had it, though, mules were loyal companions, faithful and true. More so than any horse or even dog. Carla told me that working with a mule took creativity, finesse, and patience. Bush had all of those things.

The things Bush trained Mule to do said even more about his personality. Originally used to pull the bull-tongue plow Bush used, Mule was also trained to entertain. Bush was quoted in the Knoxville News after his funeral, remarking how many people had come to see Mule "cut up," i.e. make people laugh.

Mule was a jokester. The Knoxville News-Sentinel described Mule doing all kinds of stunts at simple voice commands. They included laying down, getting up and then laying down on the other side, walking away, stopping, turning around, getting a drink, and running in a circle. It also described Mule coming out and going into her stall on command.[58] None of this sounded particularly impressive. We had a dog that could do that, except for the bit about pulling a plow, and if we put a steak in front of his nose, I bet he could have pulled a Winnebago. But that was a dog. Anyone can train a dog. Bush did an awful lot of work to train Mule to do these things, and it was an exceptional accomplishment that revealed not only his persistence, but his love of a good joke.

Bush was a born entertainer. He loved to make people laugh with his folksy, self- deprecating sense of humor. Both of the major newspapers mentioned Bush's love of jokes, but they were often at the end of stories. His sense of humor was an afterthought to the press, but it was central to his character. He was a jokester, but sadly, only his close friends and family were around to listen. Mule would listen, too, but most other people whispered accusations as he walked by, never giving him the chance to make them laugh. Being ostracized must have been excruciating for a man with an entertainer's soul.

Though Bush was a better guy than John Harvey or Don's family thought, and had not done anything of the things of which they had accused him, he himself admitted that there were things he had done that he should not have.[59] A few things were obvious. First and foremost, he did enjoy his moonshine, and it was illegal during much of his life. Moonshine is hard liquor, typically home-brewed, that is distilled from corn. Folks in Tennessee have been making and drinking it so long that it has a prominent place in "Rocky Top," the unofficial theme song of Tennessee. The line is

> Corn won't grow at all on Rocky Top,
>
> the dirt's too rocky by far.
>
> That's why all the folks on Rocky Top
>
> get their corn from a jar.

Bush was just one of many who drank it. In fact, for Beth's whole life, her uncles on her Dad's side could get moonshine almost whenever they wanted it. During summers they would pass around a Mason jar that someone had gotten from somewhere. Several people told me it tasted like a hot poker. Carla Hawkinson told me that if you dissolved one piece of rock candy in moonshine each day for fourteen days, it was be tolerable. When I heard that 'tolerable' was an improvement, I figured Tennessee moonshine had to be vile. I had been given a chance to try some West Virginia moonshine years before, but I hadn't been able to get it past my nose. I had lifted it to my face, gotten a whiff of toxic fumes that reminded me of paint thinner, and my stomach had revolted. Ever since that failure, I had been trying to redeem my manhood, but it seemed like the only time Beth's uncles couldn't get it was when we were up for a visit.

Then, one year, Beth's Uncle Bill pulled me aside at the family Christmas party. Like Tree, Bill was a tall, broad man, only with glasses and a horseshoe of graying hair. He had a huge grin on his face.

"Scott," he said, "I've got something for your bar."

"My bar?" I asked.

Bill nodded.

"My bar that I don't have?"

Bill nodded again, grinning broadly. I followed him into a back bedroom. When I stepped into the room, he was holding out a thirty-two ounce Ball Jar with what looked like preserved cherries in it.

"Now this is cherry moonshine," he said, handing it over. The moonshine was only slightly red, and the cherries were faded and dull. On the lid was a sticker with two dates. The first was the date on which it had been jarred, six months past. The second was the date on which it would be ready to drink, and it was several weeks ago. The label had been made on someone's home printer. I must have looked skeptical.

"I got this from a real moonshiner," Bill added. "I got eight jars."

"And you're giving one to me?"

Bill nodded again. My face lit up, and I gave him a huge hug. While the gift itself was amazing, it was an even better sign that I was part of the family. I took it back to Atlanta, and soon my Australian friend, Brendon, and I popped the top. If anyone could help me appreciate a new kind of liquor, it would be him.

"This is not some fake stuff," I told Brendon.

"Yeah, I can tell," he said when he got a whiff. There was no way I was going to take my first sip of moonshine out of a cup, so I lifted the jar to my face. Then I put it back down again before finally gathering my courage and taking a small sip. Brendon, who had never tasted moonshine either, watched me carefully.

It was fantastic. The moonshine tasted like a quality port, but milder. There was no "hot poker" feeling. The cherry flavor was crisp and smooth. We had planned to mix the moonshine with ginger ale to make a Tennessee Shirley Temple, but it was so good straight that we skipped the ginger ale entirely. Brendon and I, with a little help from our wives, drank the whole jar without even trying. Then we started eating the cherries. We could tell immediately that they had absorbed a good bit of the alcohol, but they were still very tasty. It didn't hit me as hard as I expected, but Beth still had to drive home. My buzz was a feeling Bush would have known well. Whether it was the cherry kind or the kind I had been unable to drink in West Virginia, it was moonshine that Bush drank when he went fox hunting with his friends, and it was a habit with complex social consequences.

For years before Bush had been born, alcohol had been a controversial topic in East Tennessee. The national move toward prohibition, called the Temperance Movement, was actually founded in Tennessee around 1800. Temperance was the belief that limiting alcohol consumption would reduce poverty, crime, violence, and all the rest of society's evils. There was more than a smidge of truth to that. Getting smashed and smashing things, including people, do sometimes go hand in hand. But the Temperance movement concluded that alcohol, as the cause of all of these problems, was itself evil. Temperance supporters thought that anyone who touched alcohol, such as Bush, had been tainted. Anyone who drank it, such as Bush, would go straight to hell. Those who actually made it were clearly in league with the Devil.

Not everyone in Tennessee was swept up in the Temperance Movement. Many swore by its medicinal value, and would drink it to cure common colds and minor ailments.[60] Folk and home remedies were common. Wild plants such as ginseng, yellow-root, witch hazel, sassafras, galax, golden-seal, and blood-root were all used as medicine.[61] Though moonshine may not have functioned as a restorative, I have no doubt that it was a highly effective painkiller, and the kind I had almost tried in West Virginia could definitely clear the sinuses. Others drank moonshine because they enjoyed the taste. It was a divisive issue throughout Bush's life.

Enough were convinced by the Temperance movement to make Tennessee the first state to pass a Prohibition law, in 1838. From that point on, it was illegal to sell alcohol in taverns and stores. It was still legal to have it, though, so people started making it themselves. This is how moonshining really became popular. More and more laws were enacted to cut away at the availability of alcohol until the state achieved what amounted to full Prohibition in 1909, making it illegal for anyone to have alcohol anywhere in the state, nine years before it became national.

National Prohibition, called "The Noble Experiment," was a failure in most respects. In one important way, though, it may well have succeeded. In 1830, the average American over age fifteen drank 7.1 gallons of alcohol per year. By 1970, the average consumption had declined to 2.5 gallons per year. Prohibition was responsible for at least some of that decrease.[62] Unfortunately, the social cost was enormous. Most people kept right on drinking alcohol, and plenty started making it. A few bootlegged it. During Prohibition, two cases of moonshine could be sold for a hundred dollars in Knoxville, about fourteen hundred 2014 dollars.[63] Moonshine was a lucrative business, but those who made or sold it were criminals. The money made from the sale of alcohol now went to them, without taxation. Meanwhile, the government was spending a fortune enforcing a law that fewer and fewer people wanted. With a sigh of relief, Tennessee joined every other state (except South Carolina) in voting to repeal Prohibition in 1933.[64]

That was not the end of the story, though. Moonshiners were reluctant to give up their home brewing. When Prohibition was repealed, taxes were applied to the purchase of legal alcohol. Moonshine remained a bargain because those who made it illegally didn't pay taxes on it. Government tax men, called "revenuers," scoured the countryside to punish those who withheld the government's cut.[65] Prohibition ended in 1933, but moonshining continued.

The Temperance movement also refused to give up. In 1939, Tennessee enacted a "local option," and each county was given the opportunity to decide for itself. The result was a patchwork of crazy laws. For instance, when I drove by the Jack Daniels Whiskey Distillery in 2003, I was shocked to find out that Jack Daniels was produced in a county where alcohol could not be consumed. So much for free samples. At that time, alcohol could not be purchased statewide on Sundays, either. Later that was changed to allow limited Sunday purchases. Georgia made the same change by public referendum, in November 2011.

Despite Prohibition's repeal and the availability of moonshine, Beth had told me, early in our relationship, that alcohol consumption was something that respectable people "just didn't do." Beth's great-granddaddy Quinn drank some, but he was from Ohio and was never a member of the upper crust of Loudon. Granddaddy, on the other hand, was a Robinson. She doesn't remember him or Mimi drinking at all. Even when they had communion at church, it was grape juice instead of wine. She still remembers being shocked the first time she saw her Uncle Larry have a beer in public. Those memories are from when temperance was at the lowest point it had ever been in Tennessee. During Bush's life it was at its peak, and Bush drank.

Enough people drank, though, that drinking was usually ignored, as long as it was kept quiet. If it went public, that was when you were in trouble. During Bush's life, drinking was the most common charge leveled against church members.[66] A typical case from the records of Cave Creek Missionary Baptist Church is an accusation made on November 4, 1908. Bill Littleton was accused of public drunkenness. A committee was formed to investigate the matter, and Littleton was forced out of the church for a time as punishment. This may not seem like a significant loss. In fact, I know some people who would enjoy being forced out of church for a while, but it was a painful blow to Littleton.

Why? Because every book I read, and every person with whom I spoke, agreed that for Bush and his community, church was the most important social connection outside of family. While not everyone went to church, most people did. Whether you were rich or poor, whether you had a suit or wore overalls, virtually everyone went to church on Sunday. The churches were divided by class, though. Mimi and Granddaddy had suits and money, so they went to the Methodist church in town, where business and community leaders attended. Poor farmers with little to spare, meanwhile, worshipped in the country churches. Though worship was segregated by class, and race, it was without a doubt the most important social connection outside of family. Bill Littleton lost that connection because of his public drunkenness.

I got another surprise when I found out that Bush himself had served on the committee that punished Bill Littleton. How could somebody who drank judge someone else for doing the same thing? The reason is simple: Bill Littleton was not punished because he had gotten drunk. He had been punished because he had been drunk in public. Bush drank, but he kept it quiet. Local records reveal that Bush was never charged with drinking by the church or the law, at a time when churches were stricter than the law. Rick had heard stories of Bush's Ridgerunner friends getting in trouble with the church, the law, and sometimes both. There were no such stories about Bush. Bush drank, and it may have given those who didn't know him further cause to dislike him, but he kept his drinking quiet. For that reason, he was in good standing at the church, and was allowed to serve on the committee to investigate Bill Littleton.

As near as I could tell, respectability in East Tennessee depended on respecting the customs rather than following them. It made sense to me that those who were respected the most never broke the rules. What I found surprising was that those who broke them quietly were still considered decent. The worst thing someone could do was not break the rules, but break them and flaunt it. Those who did not respect the rules were disrespected in return. So when it came to respectability, appearances mattered most, and Bush kept up appearances.

Which was why he was never punished for his relationship with Vine Irving.

"Bush had a girlfriend that lived with him," J.Y. McNabb told me. "Vine Irving. Little bitty woman, she used to come visit. She would spend the night with my mother. They were friends. They lived, well, I guess it was five miles from where we lived, and she would walk it."

Bush had a live-in girlfriend?

Living together before marriage isn't anything to remark about today. In Bush's day, though, it was scandalous. Living together was considered adultery, which was prohibited by the Ten Commandments from the Bible, which was taken very seriously. At night, around the fire, families would tell stories and memorize bible verses. The Ten Commandments were a popular choice. The rules of the church were strict. The story of the split in the church where Bush had his funeral shows just how strict those rules were.

During Bush's early life, there was only one church in Cave Creek: United Baptist Church. There were actually a lot of different kinds of Baptists in East Tennessee then, and most kinds survive to the present. Modern examples include General, Particular, Primitive, Up In The Spirit, Separate, Seven Day, Congregational, Southern, Missionary and just plain old Baptist. Those were just the ones Rick came up with off the top of his head. According to the Baptist World Alliance, in 2011 there were seventeen different Baptist groups, called conventions, in the United States, and two hundred eleven across the world. With over one hundred million members, Baptists were, at that time, the world's largest Protestant denomination. They were also the largest denomination in the United States, with around thirty four million members. United Baptist could not have held a hundred inside its brick walls, but it was not immune to the schism that tore the denomination apart. The seemingly minor nature of that schism shows just how seriously religion was taken during Bush's life.

The Second Great Awakening was a period of religious revival in early nineteenth century America. During this time, some Baptists became inspired to increase their mission work by being more organized and active in seeking converts. The idea of becoming more organized made quite a few people nervous. Baptists across the nation were well aware of the past persecutions of their Calvinist ancestors. A great many did not trust any authority, whether it was the government or their own denomination. They did not even trust authority within their own church, which was why pastors were seldom paid or educated and served solely at the whim of their congregation. To some, the creation of groups that would coordinate efforts sounded like a hierarchy that would eventually try to control. All of this sounded crazy to those who wanted to reach out more. They felt God calling them to go and save souls, and were offended by those who were opposed. Two camps emerged, each with their own theological reasons for their position.[67]

The group who resisted more organization became known as the Primitive Baptists Theologically, they were very conservative. They avoided anything not in the bible. Sunday School was not in the bible, so it was out. Pastors were to avoid seminary because there were no seminaries in the bible. Biblical instruction was to be done by parents, in the home, because that was how it was done in the bible. Musical instruments were not allowed in worship because the New Testament mentioned only singing. Mission work was a waste of time because God had "predestined" who would be eternally saved in heaven and who would eternally suffer in hell. Since there was no point in doing mission, there was no benefit to creating these dangerous mission boards. That was the Primitive Baptist position.[68]

Missionary Baptists did not believe that missionary work was wasted. They believed that people were not predestined for heaven or hell, but rather that everyone made a choice. The Missionary Baptists wanted everyone to end up in heaven, so they supported forming mission boards and working together. They weren't liberal, though. They were only willing to tolerate a tiny bit of change. The Primitives, on the other hand, were ultra conservative. They wanted no change at all. "I cannot change my heart," they would say. To the Missionaries, that sounded like they didn't even want to try.[69]

What became known as the Anti-Mission Split came late to United Baptist Church. The fervor of the Second Great Awakening started waning in the 1840's, but the split in United Baptist did not take place until 1869. When it finally erupted, though, it was spectacular. Elijah Breazeale, one of Bush's relatives, was a Missionary Baptist who got fed up and summoned the sheriff to have the pastor arrested over their theological and pietistic differences. That's right: arrested. The pastor, meanwhile, accused Elijah of stealing the church records. Elijah never disputed that he had them, but felt that his claim was legitimate because the pastor had gone off the deep end. No arrest was made, but this was the proverbial straw that broke the camel's back. The pastor, supported by the Harveys and other families, kept the church, adding

"Primitive" to the name. Elijah and his family left to start Cave Creek Missionary Baptist Church, eventually building their church on the other side of the same parking lot. United Baptist Church was united no longer.

Rick Holt went to Cave Creek Primitive Baptist. He described the church as being stricter than many orthodox Jewish temples. While I'm not enough of an expert on Judaism to say one way or the other, I got Rick's point that these people were serious about following the rules. For instance, a man Rick knew was accused of 'unchristian behavior,' a catchall category for anything that went against the church's strict, almost Puritan, beliefs. What heinous crime had he committed? The accusation was that the man had eaten a crawdad on a bet. The problem was not that this man had eaten a crawdad. Rather, it was that he had made a bet. That was against the rules, and it seemed to me that there were no minor rules.

If people in Cave Creek took alcohol, predestination, and gambling this seriously, then surely they would have taken adultery seriously. Sexual promiscuity was one of the most egregious sins and often had a drastic effect on social standing. Cheating on a spouse was a serious offense because illegitimate children caused personal and family disgrace.[70] Why wasn't Bush punished? Vine Irving had moved in with Bush after Bill Littleton's punishment, but why hadn't charges been brought at church? It seemed like there should have been plenty of rumors about this, but hardly anyone knew about it. John Harvey Smith had called Bush many things, but "adulterer" hadn't been on the list. None of the newspapers had reported it. In my research, I heard the name Vine Irving even less than I heard the name Brack Smith. Why hadn't word gotten out about this?

One reason was that, as has unfortunately been the case for most of human history, there was a double standard regarding sexuality. Male lust was a recognized and accepted fact of life. Men were expected to want sex outside of marriage. Even in Bush's day, young men made sexual experience a point of honor and boasting among themselves. As long as the men showed discretion and did not discuss their behavior in mixed company, their transgressions were ignored. Vine Irving probably suffered more disapproval, because women were held to a different standard. They were expected to be above all suspicion of sexual immorality. To put it bluntly, part of the reason Bush got away with it was because he was a man.[71]

The more important reason, though, was that Bush did the respectable thing. Like his drinking, he kept up appearances. He kept his relationship with Vine Irving quiet. They never went out in public as a couple. Whenever they were seen together, they behaved as if there was nothing special between them. On the surface, it seemed like there was nothing untoward going on. Bush wasn't punished for not following the moral code because he respected it.[72] He didn't always follow it, but at least he respected it. That didn't sound like a bad guy at all. It sounded like it could be anybody.

Frank Anderson gave me a wonderful summary of Bush's life. The great-grandson of Bush's sister, Delilah, Frank did extensive research into his family. Along with Rick Holt, Frank was one of my two primary sources of information about the murder of Brack Smith. Because they were local, Frank and Rick could both get court documents that I could not. I'm so grateful to both of them for their willingness to share. Frank was also my main source about Bush's life before his funeral. Before his trial, Bush had not been noteworthy. Little record of his early life remained. Other people may have known about Bush's early life, but they wouldn't talk to me. J.Y. McNabb knew some, but not much. Frank was my best link to Bush's personality before his funeral.

When we met, Frank Anderson was creeping up on sixty, of modest height, with a full head of short dark hair parted to the side. He had a round face and glasses. For over thirty years, Frank taught at the Tennessee School for the Deaf in Knoxville, a forty building private school for deaf children in kindergarten through twelfth grade. As we spoke on the campus, which looked like a college, Frank was approaching retirement. His love of family was obvious, as was his love of Bush's story. Here's what he had to say about Bush:

"The thing about parents removing their children from the street, that's probably true," Frank told me as we sat at a large conference table in a spacious meeting room. "I have heard that from other people. But then I've heard other people say, 'Why would I run from Bush Breazeale? He was my neighbor. He would sit on my porch and talk to my dad. Why would I be afraid of him?'" Frank pointed out that it all depended on the person. Anyone who did not know Bush, and who had heard only the rumors, would of course be afraid of him. For those who knew Bush well, though, he was just a regular guy, with good and bad traits alike. They knew Bush as a man who was respectful, creative, and a born jokester. To everyone else, he was the Boogeyman. It was a label he simply could not shed.

For the fifty years between Brack Smith's murder and his live funeral, Bush lived in unwanted isolation with his parents in that tiny cabin on the family farm. His sister, Hannah, who had also never married, lived there, too. Bush and Hannah's job was to take care of their aging parents. Children were expected to care for their parents as they aged because farm work was too difficult for the elderly.[73] As Bush's parents got older and older, they relied on him and Hannah more and more. They grew food for themselves in a garden and had a truck patch for crops for sale or trade.[74] When Bush needed something he couldn't grow, he traded at the store or went to Loudon. For recreation, he went night hunting one night a week with the Ridgerunners. On Sundays he went to church, where he kept his living arrangement and drinking quiet enough to be a member in good standing. Though Loudon and the rest of the country changed around him, Cave Creek and Dogwood remained largely the same. Life changed little. When it finally did, though, it propelled Bush toward the live funeral that would make him famous.

Chapter Five

The Legend Begins

Late in his life Bush lived with three people: his mother, Sarah Littleton Breazeale; his father, Drury Wood (D.W.) Breazeale; and his sister, Hannah. Like Bush, Hannah had never married. Death must have been on Bush's mind as his parents grew older and older. Despite being four years younger than her husband, Bush's mother died first, on January 4, 1921. She was ninety-four. Soon after, at ninety-eight, D.W. suffered a stroke. He died later that same year. When Vine Irving moved in, the household was back up to three. That lasted until June 4, 1937, when Hannah died. Less than a year later, in May of 1938, Vine Irving died. For the first time in his more than seventy years of life, Bush was alone.

Community was of vital importance to the people of East Tennessee, and dying alone was terrifying. Thomas Carlyle, a Scottish-born Southern writer, wrote this on the subject:

"Isolation is the sum total of wretchedness to a man. To be cut off, to be left solitary; to have a world alien, not your world, all a hostile camp for you; not a home at all, of hearts and faces who are yours, whose you are!...Without father, without child, without brother. Man knows no sadder destiny."[75]

For Bush, the prospect of dying alone was made even worse by the legacy he would leave. Legacy mattered a great deal because it was interconnected with morality. A moral failing on the part of one

member of the community was a blemish on themselves, their family, and the community as a whole.[76]
Because Bush's reputation would be a lasting stain on
the family name and on the community, I could see
why he wanted to change his legacy.

But I still wondered why he chose a live funeral.

Bush was creative and not afraid to step outside
social norms, but there are many ways for a creative
person to change their legacy. In my church work, I've
seen people who are not creative do it all the time. A
public work, such as a pew for the church, would
have been nice. Pews, stained glass windows and
pulpits are often donated to churches and the name of
the donor gets preserved for all time. At one church
where I worked, a woman donated a new steeple.
Bush also could have donated his land to some noble
cause, or he could have donated timber, or crops, or
whatever else he had. Why a live funeral?

The answer was in, of all places, Atlanta.

Mick Breazeale was a distant relative of Bush. He
maintained a genealogy website for the Mississippi
branch of the Breazeale family.[77] Because he was a distant relative, Bush's story was part of Mick's family
lore. Mick gave Bush a special section on the Mississippi Clan Breazeale website, and he and I got together several times to share pints of Blue Moon beer
and talk about Bush.

"You know who you need to meet?" Mick asked
me one day as we each started our second pint.

"Who?"

"Frank Huggins."

"Why?"

"Because he knows where Bush got the idea to have a funeral," Mick replied.

I called Frank.

Frank Huggins was a captain in the Sheriff's Department in Forsyth County, Georgia, just north of where I lived. We met one morning before work at an Atlanta Bread Company off a highway exit. Frank arrived in police uniform, with his gun and handcuffs. Tall and thin, with a horseshoe of white hair, Frank was nearing retirement at the time. His scholarly glasses and thin white moustache gave him a distinguished appearance, like a college professor. Soon after we met, he took the retirement plunge and started riding his Harley Davidson motorcycle all over the South. There was a hint of East Tennessee in Frank's accent because he was born in Kingston, though he had moved away while still young. The man responsible for the family moving to Kingston was Frank's grandfather, Augustus Summers.

"I believe my grandfather is the one who gave Bush the idea to have a live funeral," Frank said. Bush and Summers had been good friends, perhaps because Summers was also an outsider. Born in Eminence, Indiana, on January 14, 1888, Summers was a Yankee. He had moved with his wife, Berta, to Kingston and bought the Kingston Banner newspaper. Later, he renamed it the Roane County Banner to broaden appeal. For an outsider in East Tennessee, owning a newspaper would have had its fair share of challenges. There were certain ways of saying things in East Tennessee, and often the words had no obvious surface connection to their actual meaning. The phrase "low down" is just one example of "what you say," and only if you knew the code did you know what was meant.

As another example, when Rick Holt and I were riding back from Bush's house I offered to buy him lunch. Rick didn't say anything at first, but as we pulled up to his car he finally spoke.

"I reckon I about wore you out," Rick told me. Whether I was worn out or not had nothing to do with it. That was Rick's way of saying, "I'm outta here." Another example came during a later phone conversation.

"Well, I know you're busy," Rick said after our business had concluded. That was a polite way of saying, "I'm done talking to you." It was a miracle, but I got the hint both times. Beth must have been doing something right.

Those were innocuous examples, but plenty were not so nice. A popular Southern expression is "Bless your heart." I always thought it sounded nice, until Beth explained it to me one day.

"So it means 'You're an idiot and I feel sorry for you?'" I asked her.

"Not really," she said. "But close enough." Quite a few Southern expressions that sound nice really aren't. In New York I was raised to say what I meant, and to mean what I said. I sometimes got lost in conversations with Southerners.

Augustus Summers was from the Midwest, but that still made him a Yankee, and local language and culture were potential minefields. Church rules were so strict that if he cast an unfair aspersion, even unintentionally, he faced sanctions. Anytime he criticized anyone, he would eventually have to face not just that person, but their immediate and distant family. It would have been impossible to avoid. Despite the challenges, Summers seems to have done well. He wrote what needed to be written without making enemies. It was quite an accomplishment for a Yankee, and one I hoped to emulate.

Summers was twenty-eight years younger than Bush, and his opposite in several ways. He was about five and a half feet tall, with wire-rimmed glasses perched over round eyes. A buzz-cut horseshoe of hair topped a clean-shaven face, giving him an academic look. Bush, on the other hand, was barely over five feet tall, slightly below average. He had a white comb-over and half a foot of bushy white beard. Bush had never been to school, while Summers had several college degrees that he never used. Dogwood was the only home Bush had ever known, and farming was his only job. Summers never lived anywhere for long, including Kingston, and changed jobs frequently. Marriage and family suited Summers, who had four daughters: Agnes, Frida, Olive and Helen. Bush, on the other hand, had never married nor had children. The two men seemed so very different, and yet they were good friends. Huggins showed me a great picture of Bush, Summers, and another man out to lunch in Kingston. They were all seated around the table looking at the menu, as familiar and as different as can be.

Picture courtesy Frank Huggins, grandson of Augustus Summers

A. Summers   Mike

Uncle Bush dining out with his 'publicity agent', Augustus Summers, and a friend.

Huggins. Date unknown

What brought Summers and Bush together was their love of storytelling. They regaled one another with stories about the things they had done, the people they had outwitted, and the jokes they had played. Each man found the other wildly entertaining, and they spent a lot of time swapping stories and laughing. They were two peas in a pod, but these traits led to some conflict at home for Summers. Berta, his wife, was forced to run the house because he wouldn't. She disciplined the children while Summers played and laughed with them. His relationship with his children and grandchildren was more friend and jokester than disciplinarian, and he and Berta did not see eye to eye on how to raise their family. Frank

Huggins said that he "could not imagine his grandfather disciplining him," but he clearly remembers Summers letting him drive the car at age six. Augustus Summers, like his good friend Bush Breazeale, enjoyed nothing better than entertaining people. They were good friends.

One typical Summers story took place after he left Kingston. After selling his newspaper and leaving Kingston, he took his family to Florida. With no job or income, they ended up camping along the dirt roads outside Gainesville. One day, Summers went into the Gainesville Courthouse to look for a job. He came out whistling, having just been hired as Superintendent of Schools. That was Augustus Summers: a man who could walk into a building where no one knew him and come out in charge of all their children. It's a good thing he was a nice guy.

The story Huggins told me over coffee was that in the fall of 1937, Bush and Summers were chewing the fat behind Bush's house. Summers was smoking his trademark Pall Mall filterless cigarettes when he looked over at the big walnut tree next to the back corner of the house. It was about two feet in diameter, tall and straight. Walnut was very valuable. Summers, always looking for ways to make a quick buck, asked Bush what he planned to do with the tree.

"Gonna make my coffin out of it," Bush told him. Walnut was often used in the construction of coffins, and making your own coffin was a relatively common practice.[78]

From there the conversation turned to funerals, death and legacy. Summers observed that it was a shame that we never know what is said about us at our funeral. He might not have known what people would say about him, but Bush sure did. Bush realized that at his funeral people were going to say that he was a murderer and a thief. They might even say that he was a moonshiner and an adulterer. He realized that his legacy was not his own, and time was running out to change it.

The Walnut Stump - Author's collection,

Not long after this conversation, Bush decided that a live funeral would show people the truth about him. He wanted to be sure that the good things about him were said publicly, for all to hear, by a minister. Ministers had status because the church, effectively, was the community. If the church approved of a minister, then the community did as well, and that meant that the minister's words could be trusted.[79] If people heard the truth from a minister, they would change their minds. They would see that he was not the man they thought he was, and he could be known for who he really was. Holding it while he was still alive was the only way to control what was said. It would clear the air, and his name, so he could finally die as a member in good standing and leave behind a worthwhile legacy. So Bush decided to have his funeral while he was still alive.[80]

Bush got to work on that walnut tree. To hew the trunk, he used a long, two-handed logging saw.[81] A handle at each end, it was meant to be used by two people, but Bush did all the sawing himself. I was told by an expert that this was not possible, but Bush did it. The saw was six or eight feet long, flexible, and the handles were each big enough for two hands to grasp. Bush pulled and pushed it horizontally across the trunk, back and forth. When I cut down trees, I cut the stump close to the ground. This stump was three feet high, to make it easier for him to move the saw. Once most of the trunk had been cut through with the saw, it was felled with an axe.

After the tree fell, Bush used that same two handled saw to cut the trunk into logs. Then, Mule dragged the logs to the lumber mill of J. M. Cook, where the tree was sawed into one-inch thick boards. Over the winter of 1937-38, Bush used these boards to make his coffin. Pictures show that it was simple, all flat lines and edges, not a curve to be found.

Huggins, 1938

Both of the end boards were slightly wider at the top, so that while the coffin looked rectangular from the side, from the end it looked like a trapezoid, with the wider part on top. It was also wider at the waist than at the head or foot. The top, bottom, sides and ends were each made of only one piece of wood. The lid was flat and unadorned, just like the rest of the coffin. On the front, Bush inscribed the words "At Rest."[82] The entire coffin was stained and polished to a shine.

Making the coffin took about a year. According to a 1958 Knoxville News-Sentinel article, Bush then took the casket to Berry's Funeral Home in Knoxville, which lined it and fitted it. When it was finished, Bush was ready to begin planning his live funeral.

In the spring of 1938, he went to the funeral home closest to his home, Quinn Funeral Home in Loudon. To get there he needed to cross the wide, slow Tennessee River. There were two ferries. The first was the one in Cave Creek, near the store. Its name has been lost, and there is some debate as to whether that ferry was operating at the time. There was definitely another ferry he could have taken, though. That one, which ran due east, in the direction of Knoxville and Lenoir City, was Blair's Ferry, also called Loudon Ferry, the impetus behind the founding of Loudon. It remained in operation until 1948.[83] Taking Blair's Ferry would have meant an extra mile or two, but even so it would have taken only an afternoon to get there and back. Bush took one of these ferries to Loudon. It was a trip he had taken many times during his life.

Until recently, ferries were a fixture in Tennessee. According to the Tennessee Encyclopedia of History and Culture, the state has over a thousand miles of navigable waterways and over nineteen thousand miles of streams. Tennessee was first settled along its rivers: Knoxville and Chattanooga along the Tennessee, Memphis along the Mississippi, and Nashville along the Cumberland. Ferries were vital crossings along major transportation routes, and were significant landmarks. Today that part is played by bridges, but large-scale bridge construction did not begin until around 1900. Even then, the first bridges were naturally built in major population centers, which Loudon was not. By 1938, in fact, many of the thousand ferries that once existed in Tennessee had vanished, but it still was how Bush got to Loudon.

Ferries back then consisted of a dock on either bank of the river, a flat-bottomed barge, and a thick rope. On both ends of the barge were big eye holes with pulleys. The rope passed through the eye holes, connecting the barge to both docks. Passengers would board at either dock and pay a fee based on their cargo. The more cargo you had, the more your fare. There was room for horses, mules, even a wagon or two. Slack was left in the rope, so that no matter from which side of the river the ferry departed, the current pushed the barge downstream and across the river. Enough momentum was built up by the river itself that only at the very end of the trip did the ferryman have to pull on the rope.

No matter which ferry Bush took, it was not long before he was in Loudon, where in 1916, Beth's great-granddaddy, Frank Quinn, had opened Quinn Funeral Home. Born in Hardin, Ohio, on January 2, 1887, Quinn had been told by a friend from Loudon that they could use a funeral home down there. Quinn said "Sure," packed up the family, and moved to Loudon to start it. While I would be scared to death at the idea of starting a business in a small town where I barely knew anyone, Quinn was never afraid of anything, even to a fault.

The job Frank Quinn left behind in Dayton, Ohio was commemorated on a plaque treasured by Beth's family. Mimi was Quinn's daughter, and she displayed that plaque in a prominent place on a hallway wall. On top was a picture of a group of men. On the bottom was a large pair of canvas shears. The picture was from 1908, and it was of Frank Quinn, several other men, and the famous Wright Brothers, Orville and Wilbur. It was taken five years after their historic flight at Kitty Hawk. The scissors had been used to cut the fabric for their Model B airplane, which Frank Quinn had helped design and build. The Model B was the fifth generation of plane descended from the Wright Flyer I flown at Kitty Hawk. After that came the Flyer II and III, which were experimental. The Model A was the first commercial aircraft in the world. With Quinn's help, the Model A was improved, and evolved into the Model B, which was released in 1910 and sold to both the public and the government.[84] While he was working on the Model B, Mimi was born. Given the name Kathryn, she was only two when they moved to Loudon. Her sister, Eleanor ("Pete"), was born soon after they moved, in 1915. He operated the funeral home successfully for many years, and it has operated continuously ever since.

Modern funeral homes are built specifically for the purpose for which they are intended. They have designed offices, a chapel, visitation rooms and a carport. Quinn Funeral Home, on the other hand, was founded in an actual home just past the Baptist church. The two-story brick front had three windows on the top floor and two on the bottom. A door opened in the middle of a full-length porch. Inside the door was a burgundy foyer, with offices to the right and a small sitting room to the left. Straight ahead, through a short hallway, was the chapel. Painted a soothing white, the chapel was a later addition. With chairs in rows, fifty people could squeeze in.

Frank Quinn did well in Loudon. He was a pioneer in embalming in Tennessee, eventually rising to head of the Tennessee State Embalmers Association, a position he held for many years. Through it, he made some powerful friends, most notably Governor Frank Clement and United States Senator Estes Kefauver. At various times he held leadership positions in the local and state Masonic organizations, his Methodist church, and the local Methodist district. Though he was not ordained, churches in East Tennessee would occasionally invite him to speak during their Sunday services.

Being the only funeral director in town meant more than just directing funerals. Loudon was a center of trade, but it was too small to have its own ambulance. Most trucks had open beds, and were dangerous and unsanitary, since they were used for hauling all sorts of things. Cars of the day were small, cramped, and would have done more harm than good if someone was seriously injured. Believe it or not, the best vehicle in town for delivering injured people to the hospital was Quinn's hearse. It was clean, enclosed, and had plenty of room in the back. Frank Quinn was both funeral director and ambulance driver. He would drive the sick and injured to the hospital in Loudon or to the bigger facilities in Knoxville. I can only imagine what it must have felt like to be taken to the hospital in a hearse. It was probably small comfort to know that if things went wrong, the undertaker was already there.

There was a great story Beth's uncles liked to tell about how Quinn came upon a car wreck that had just happened and loaded the dazed man into the hearse. When the man woke up in the hearse, he thought he was a goner.

"Mr. Quinn," he asked, "how'd you get here so fast?"

Quinn made plenty of jokes about that and everything else, usually with a cigar in his hand. For a time, he carried a pair of false teeth around town, telling people he had just pulled them from a dead body, asking if anyone needed them. He was also well known for his horn-rimmed glasses and a love of fine suits. At the time of Bush's funeral, he kept his hair short and parted to the side, though later in life he had a buzz cut. Children knew him for his harmonica playing and jokes. Teens knew him by his amazing ability to ride a bicycle backwards. Men knew him as the best gripper in town; that's when two men grab hands in a handshake and squeeze until someone can't take it anymore. The muscles he had developed stretching canvas over wings for the Wright Brothers never weakened, even in his old age. Frank Quinn was, as Steve put it, "larger than life."

Though the funeral home was well established when Bush arrived, at the time it was struggling.

"In 1931," said Uncle Steve, "the banks went bust all over the country, and in the Loudon area, the banks went bust, too. My grandfather [Frank Quinn] had his money in one of the local banks. It went belly up, he didn't get any money out, and he didn't have any money anymore. All his money was gone. So he went to see some of the prominent, wealthy businessmen in town, and he put together a deal with them, whereby they would loan him enough money to keep up his inventory of caskets and equipment and so forth, and keep the funeral home business going. They didn't want the funeral home to go out of business, and they, in turn, would get a share of the funeral home. They would hold that share and the profits would be divided among them until he had paid them back completely. Once he did, the contract was null and void. So, before and during the time of Bush's funeral, he was in debt to these guys."

The note was a ten year loan held by three prominent local men. Over that time, these men would take twenty-five percent of funeral home profits until the loan was paid off. One of the men was named McQuerry, and he was from nearby Sweetwater. The second was Don. P. Smith, who had purchased a chair factory in Loudon in 1922. Barksdale Greer was the third investor. He was a member of the prominent Greer family and co-owner of Greer's Hardware. Greer's had existed since 1890 and is still in business. It is a Loudon institution, and their help gave Quinn the support of a powerful family during a difficult time.

As part of the loan agreement, Quinn worked at Greer's Hardware. His responsibilities included those of furniture buyer, but he was best known for running the Saturday morning auctions. On Saturday mornings, Greer's would auction off things that were not selling. People from all over the county and beyond would come and bid, hoping to get a deal. Frank Quinn knew how to gather a crowd: by giving things away. Usually it was something for an expectant mother, or newlyweds, or some needy person he knew could not afford to bid.

While Quinn loved to be the center of attention, he also enjoyed helping behind the scenes. Sometimes he would slip "farm aids" into the pockets of unsuspecting businessmen in Loudon. These were small amounts of cash to help a struggling business get by. Granddaddy used to say that no one in Loudon County had anonymously given away more to help others than Frank Quinn. That may be why he agreed to put on Bush's funeral.

Funerals cost hundreds of dollars back then, but Bush did not have even ten dollars. There was no way he could pay for a funeral. He wasn't asking for much because he figured only twenty or thirty people would attend, but it was still more than he could afford. It was unorthodox, and Frank Quinn would not make any money, but it was an opportunity to help someone in need. Quinn probably didn't even know what Bush was in need of, but it didn't matter. Besides, the funeral wouldn't take much effort. It would just be a short, simple service. There wouldn't even be a burial. Quinn saw a chance to lend a hand to someone who needed it, and it sounded like an adventure. He jumped right in. Quinn Funeral Home staff member Frank "Buddy" Robinson, the man Beth would later call Granddaddy, followed suit.

The Live Funeral of Uncle Felix "Bush" Breazeale was scheduled for June 26, 1938, at 2:00 p.m. Bush was a member of Cave Creek Primitive Baptist Church, so they would host. It would take a crowd to change his public image, so Bush planned the funeral for early summer. Funerals were occasionally delayed for that long so distant relatives or friends could attend, and this gave him three or four months to invite everyone he knew. People Bush knew well, people he barely knew at all, it didn't matter. When he went to Loudon, he told people there. When he went to Kingston, he told people there. Everyone, everywhere, got an invitation. Bush figured that if he invited enough people, he just might get thirty to actually show up. That, he hoped, would be enough to clear his name and reputation.

After Bush told a few people, curiosity slowly began to grow. They wondered what you did at a live funeral. Would it be like a real funeral? Would there be singing? Who would the preacher be? They also wondered about what would happen before and after. Would there be visitation before? Would there be a reception after? They wondered what Bush would do. Would he lie in the coffin? Or would he sit nearby?

Finally, and most importantly, they wondered what would be said. Sermons and eulogies were, and are, one of the most important parts of a funeral. What would the preacher say, and would Bush give his own eulogy? If he did, would he say why he was having his funeral while he was still alive? The few remaining people in Cave Creek who knew about the murder of Brack Smith wondered if he planned to confess. People who had known Bush their whole lives joined those across the county in wondering the same thing I had: why was he having a live funeral? The mystery added to the anticipation.

Over the next month, word spread out from Loudon and Kingston and into the surrounding countryside. The story bubbled forth, and more and more people who were talking about the funeral did not know Bush directly. In such a highly religious and moral culture, people must have wanted to know if this funeral was going to be respectable. In order to find out, they used the same method Ham Carey used on me when we first met at McGill-Karnes Funeral Home.

Beth told me that, though she's known Ham all her life, she had no idea what his real first name is. Three years later, I found out that it was Hamill. Around age eighty when we first met, Ham introduced himself as a newcomer to Loudon, having moved there from Memphis fifty five years before. Ham had married the daughter of a Greer and had taken over Greer's Hardware. After Ham retired, his son took over. When Ham and I first met, it took all of five minutes for him to bring up family.

"Let me address something one quick second," he asked, apropos of nothing. "S-E-E-K-E, what kind of name is that?"

"German," I answered.

"German?"

"German. It was originally von Seeke." Unfortunately, he didn't seem impressed that I was descended from nobility. No one ever was. "They're from the northern coast of Germany, a town called Wilhelmshaven."

"When did they come over?" Ham wondered. My dad had recently begun researching family history, so I actually had some answers.

"They came over in the late 1800's, just before the turn of the century. The only thing I have from my family on my dad's side is a picture from Germany, from the late 1800's, of some men on a ship. Von Seeke means 'of the sea.'"

"Ok!" To Ham, it seemed we were now getting somewhere.

"So they were seafaring captains," I continued, "and there were six guys in the picture, but I don't know which guy in the picture I'm related to. All I've got is a list of names. I know that my son is the sixth generation of Seeke with the name 'John' in there somewhere."

"Alright." The conversation drifted to other things, but somehow Ham worked the conversation back to family. This time he wondered about my mom, and where I was raised.

"Where did you grow up?" Ham asked. "Where's your mom? Tell me about that."

"My mom lives in Florida now. My grandmother moved down in 1980…"

"From the Atlanta area?"

"From New York."

"Oh." I thought that Atlanta may have been a better answer.

"Six months after they moved," I continued, "my grandfather died. She stayed down there fifteen, sixteen years, and then she got emphysema...and she reached a point where she couldn't take care of herself. So my parents said 'Well, we can move her up here, or we can move down there.' So they sold the house and moved down, a quarter mile from her, and they took care of her the last seven years of her life." I think Ham approved.

While it may seem like Ham was being nosy, he was not. All of this took place in the context of a long, pleasant conversation. But as Beth and I talked about that conversation, I realized how often this type of conversation took place. For instance, when Beth dated someone new in high school, Granddaddy would ask about who his people were.

"You can't change your family," he would say.

More than any other place I have ever been, people in East Tennessee want to find out who your people are so they can know who you are. Family was another form of classism, and it may have been the most important one of all.

Once the area was settled, few people moved into Loudon and Cave Creek, and few moved out. If they moved, it was a local move. Because the families seldom changed, patterns of behavior emerged. Respectable living seemed to run in families, as did character. People who lived respectably tended to have children and grandchildren who lived respectably. People with good character tended to have children and grandchildren of good character. The opposite was also true. Some families just seemed full of rotten apples. When getting to know someone in East Tennessee, their family often provided a barometer of what to expect.[85]

Family also set the pecking order in East Tennessee society. The Robinson family was well respected for generations in Loudon. For a long time, I thought that their status outweighed their contribution. It wasn't that they had never done anything important. For decades they had owned the Robinson Mill, a grist mill that had been vital in a farming community. As farming declined, they shifted occupations. Frank Smith Robinson, Sr., Granddaddy's father, was a contractor who built many of the homes in modern Loudon. He also ran the pipeline that brought the city its first central water system. Before that, everyone in town had their own well. Running the grist mill, bringing water, and building homes are certainly important contributions, but I got the sense that there was more to it than that.

It turned out that I was right.

The status of the Robinson family did not primarily derive from their many accomplishments. Instead, their status, and the status of the other prominent families, came from nothing more than the fact that they had been there the longest.

I discovered this when I interviewed two former mayors of Loudon, Harold Amburn and Gene Lambert. Tree had set up the meeting. Former Mayor Inky Swiney was supposed to be there, but he had just had a stroke seven days before. Even though Renee

McGill's sister had just spotted him smoking in his car port the day before our meeting, he elected to skip it. I can't say I blamed him. Steve came along, as did Ham, who was the head of the Loudon County Historical Society. The purpose of the meeting was for them to tell me about Loudon history.

At that time, little of the history of Loudon had been written. It existed primarily in the stories of the people that lived there. To learn that history, I sat and listened to these four old guys spin yarns for three hours.[86] They did so without a pause or a break. I had brought them biscuits from Hardee's, but they ate slowly. They only took a bite when someone else was telling a story. After each bite, they set the biscuit back down. It would be several minutes before they took another bite. The conversation moved from story to story. One would end and someone would just start the next one. In their minds the stories were probably connected, but it was often difficult to tell how. Name after name came up. During the first five minutes of our conversation, I wrote down how many stories they told and how many people they mentioned. In just those five minutes, they told six stories and mentioned nineteen different people.

"We're supposed to be telling you history and here we are just talkin'," Ham said after an hour and a half.

"You are telling me history," I told him, because they were. East Tennessee was an oral culture. That was how its history was passed on. It wasn't in books or articles. It was passed on by telling stories, and these old guys were full of them.

During that three hour conversation, the same names kept coming up. I kept hearing stories about the Greers, Simpsons, Blairs, Carmichaels, Robinsons (a few of whom were named Roberson), Johnstons and Harrisons. There were other prominent families at different times, but these families were the cream of the crop. The Carmichaels and Blairs were the earliest settlers, the ones who built the ferry and inn on the opposite side of the river. The others all came at the time of the Hiwassee land sale in 1819 or 1820. Each family had an identity and played a part in the community.

"The Simpsons were always smart," my mother-in-law told me when I asked her about them. The Simpsons lived north of Loudon, near the Harrisons, who were doctors. One famous Harrison, Dr. Joe Harrison, was known for having had a pet monkey. The Johnstons laid out what would become Loudon, but they were also known for owning a saw mill and a grocery. The Robinsons owned the grist mill, while the Greers owned the store. These families made other important contributions, such as those made by Granddaddy's father. More than any particular event or achievement, though, these families were prominent because of the sum of their parts. They had been good, honest people for generations. They were respected because there was a hundred years' evidence that they were respectable. They were trusted because there was a hundred years of evidence that they were trustworthy. And because they had been there the longest.

So when East Tennesseans outside Cave Creek started hearing about the funeral, one of the first questions they had was who this Bush guy was, and whether he was trustworthy. The way they found out was to ask about his people. They didn't have to look far. Breazeales were all over East Tennessee. Beth had even gone to school with some.

The Breazeales of East Tennessee were descended from Henry Breazeale, who came in 1790. He had two brothers; one of them settled in the middle of Mississippi, the other in Louisiana. All three branches of the family are still going strong. Not all of Bush's family was poor, either. Bush's great-grandfather, Willis Breazeale, had been a doctor. Bush's nephew, T. M. Breazeale, was City Attorney of Lenoir City and one of the partners in the law firm Breazeale & Breazeale. Sam Breazeale, a distant relative, was an attorney in Harriman and became a state senator. On Bush's mother's side were more attorneys, including one branch of the family that entered the upper crust of American society.

Martin Littleton was born in Roane County, but moved first to Texas and then to New York, eventually becoming a United States Representative. Martin's sister, Rachel, married Cornelius Vanderbilt IV in 1919, linking Bush to the Vanderbilts, one of the wealthiest and most influential families in the country. The marriage ended in divorce in 1927, but Rachel went on to marry one of J.P. Morgan's nephews. The

The Littleton Mausoleum - Friends of the Woodlawn Cemetery, 2015. Woodlawn Cemetery, Bronx, NY

Littletons were prominent in New York City, and Martin and Rachel are both buried in a mausoleum in Woodlawn Cemetery in the Bronx. Their mausoleum is across the cemetery from where several of my Seeke ancestors are buried.

Anyone who did not know Bush would have asked about his family. They would have soon found out that, despite being a poor farmer, he came from a respected local family, from "good people." For that reason, strangers trusted that this bizarre event would be, at the very least, proper and not a farce. Confidence grew that nothing embarrassing or untoward would happen. Those who still wondered no doubt looked to the prominent families for guidance. People who lived in Cave Creek looked to their leaders, and people in Loudon looked to theirs. The reaction of most of Loudon's prominent citizens seems to have been muted. Quinn was well connected, but his opinions lacked the necessary clout. Instead, the most important person to support the funeral may have been none other than Granddaddy.

Granddaddy, whom everyone called Buddy, worked at Quinn Funeral Home. Though he was only twenty four at the time of Bush's funeral, the Robinson family reputation was safe in Granddaddy's hands. As a child, he had been well known for his love of sports and art. Throughout his life he drew and painted. We have one of his paintings on our wall, a beautiful landscape with mountains and a river. Though his paintings were wonderful, he was best known for his cartoons. Just about everyone I've met in Loudon has a cartoon he sent them. When I met with the former mayors of Loudon, Ham Carey brought one of Granddaddy's cartoons. He sent them to people to celebrate the good times, bring comfort in the bad times, and sometimes just because the mood struck him.

Granddaddy was a runner before running was cool. "Running an errand" is a figure of speech, but Granddaddy actually did it. He would run all around Loudon as a child. When he was in school in the 1920's, a boy could only try out for varsity sports in the seventh grade. Granddaddy was the only person in Loudon, and the only one I've heard of anywhere, who lettered in football for six seasons. Though he was a great runner, he played on the offensive line.

Granddaddy graduated from Loudon High School in 1932. That was the height of the Great Depression, and jobs were hard to find. One of the main employers in town was the Bacon Hosiery Mill, owned by the richest man in town, Colonel Charles H. Bacon. Colonel was an honorary title given to prominent citizens by the governor, and Col. Bacon was more than just owner of the Hosiery Mill. He was also owner of a cotton mill, president and director of the 1st National Bank of Loudon, and director of two businesses in Chattanooga. Earlier in his career, he had owned mills in Greenville, Newport and Sevierville. His biggest business was the Bacon Hosiery Mill in Loudon, which employed a thousand people.[87] Granddaddy decided to get a job there.

One Monday morning, Granddaddy went to see the Hosiery Mill President, Mr. Kirkland. He was politely told that there were no jobs available, so he left. On Tuesday morning, he met Mr. Kirkland as he was entering the mill, and told him that he was going to fill out an application and go to work. Mr. Kirkland again politely explained that there were no jobs to be had. Granddaddy thanked him and left. The same scene took place every day that week, with Mr. Kirkland getting more and more frustrated and rude. By Friday he was fed up.

"What must I do to convince you that we cannot afford to hire anyone at this time?" he asked. Granddaddy replied that he didn't have to pay him.

"I'll work for free until you feel I'm productive enough to be paid," he said. Mr. Kirkland stared at him for a full moment and then turned to his secretary.

"Louise, let this young man fill out an application. If we don't hire him, Buddy Robinson will drive me completely crazy."

Granddaddy was known as Buddy, and Mimi was known as Kat, short for Katherine. She was the oldest of Quinn's two daughters. After Buddy and Kat were married, on February 23, 1935, Quinn extended a job offer to his new son-in-law. Granddaddy could learn the undertaking profession, assisting Quinn. Someday, if he chose, Granddaddy might take over the business. This was what led him to assist Quinn in providing Bush with his live funeral, and to the funeral getting the seal of approval from the important Robinson family. If Granddaddy approved, then the Robinsons approved. If the Robinsons approved, it would respectable. People in Loudon and across the area started making plans to attend, and excitement grew.

What never came up was the murder of Brack Smith. No one outside of Cave Creek knew anything about it. A few in Cave Creek, such as John Harvey Smith's family, did know, but they did not get the word out. It called to mind a story that my mother-in-law once told me about Granddaddy. In the 1990's, someone in Loudon had been having strange things happen in their home. They thought the house might be haunted. One of the Knoxville television stations got wind of the possible haunting and did a story on it. Granddaddy was furious. It was the only time I had heard that word used to describe him.

"Some things," he fumed, "should not be told."

Cave Creek kept the story of Brack Smith's murder to itself because it was a stain on their community. Even though the killing had been sanctioned, it was not something about which people outside the community needed to know. Those who knew about the murder kept it to themselves, sometimes even keeping it from people in their own community. Why? Because some things should not be told.

Two months before Bush's funeral, Augustus Summers realized that the story of Bush's live funeral was moving faster than he could keep up with it, a dilemma with which he was familiar. The local rumor mill often moved faster than the newspaper. For that reason, how Summers reported the news often mattered more than when. Newspapers had a voice of authority. They were trusted. Summers had the role of a local Walter Cronkite, giving an unofficial stamp of approval to events most people already knew about. I do not believe Summers ran the story announcing Bush's live funeral in the Roane County Banner so people could find out about it, because they probably already knew. I believe he ran it to encourage people to attend. He also made sure they had the correct information, printing when and where, and probably selling a fair number of newspapers in the process. With the approval of prominent community leaders, a church, and a newspaper, funeral buzz grew.

Then Summers took a leap.

The locals were so excited that Summers wondered if people outside East Tennessee might be as interested. They might, he thought. They just might.

So, for perhaps the only time in his news career, Summers sent out a press release to both of the major wire services, the Associated Press (A.P.) and United Press International (U.P.I.). The release was picked up by The Knoxville News-Sentinel, which ran it on May 1, 1938, almost two full months before the funeral. The headline read "Aged Man to Hear His Own Funeral." The subhead was "Roane Countian Makes Coffin: Faithful Mule to Pull It." It's quite the attention grabber, and the article itself does not disappoint. It shares details about the casket, Bush, Mule, and about Bush's desire to "have the true facts" given about himself. Like everyone else who heard about the funeral, people in Knoxville ate it up.

Over the next several weeks the story appeared in other, distant places that had never heard of Cave Creek. It ran in Nashville, and in newspapers outside of Tennessee. Not every paper carried it, but many did. People across the country were asking the same questions as people in Loudon, Kingston and Cave Creek:

Why did Bush want to have a live funeral?

No one knew, but they thought that if they came, they just might find out.

Chapter Six

The Legend Builds

Most people I've met think ministers do most of the work of putting on a funeral. In a church funeral, we do quite a bit, but even then, the majority of the work is often done by the funeral director. I write a sermon, lead the service, and comfort the family both before and after. To make all that go smoothly, a lot of work needs to be done behind the scenes, and most of that is done by the funeral director. In Bush's case, as with many funerals, the six staff of Quinn Funeral Home (Quinn, Granddaddy, and four others) were responsible for planning the service, printing the programs, setting up the tent, arranging transportation, lining up the singers and preachers, and, if needed, renting a public address system. The funeral rested squarely on their shoulders.

For some people, the pressure of such a popular event would have been too much, but Frank Quinn dealt with pressure at every funeral. Each one is a milestone, and people remember the funeral of a loved one for the rest of their lives. The last thing the funeral director wants is to be remembered for dropping the casket or playing the wrong song instead of "the one that grandma loved best of all." At one funeral I led, the director used the wrong name for the deceased. He wasn't going to recover from that one, and after the funeral was over, that was what everyone talked about. No one remembered the eulogy, the music, or even my amazing sermon.

Rather than be intimidated by the growing expectations and pressure, Quinn thrived on them. He loved pressured moments. The key to his success was hard work and attention to detail. Success, he had learned, did not come from taking shortcuts. This lesson was passed on to his children and grandchildren. While Augustus Summers spoiled his grandchildren, Frank Quinn gave his an education. The few times he played cards for money with his little granddaughter, Beth's mom, he took her for everything she had. To her great surprise, he kept it, even though she was just a child. She quickly learned that there were no shortcuts in life, and still does not like to gamble.

Quinn also knew that success required that he be stubborn and exacting with everyone leading a funeral. When one small mistake can mean disaster, the only way to ensure success is to ensure that there aren't any mistakes. Quinn demanded excellence, and was successful because he got it. Every detail of each funeral was drilled into his employees to ensure that everything went properly. The minister, the florist, the soloist, and all the other participants were thoroughly coached on how to conduct themselves. I'm sure more than one bristled, but Quinn knew what he was doing. That was how he stayed in business so long, and how he garnered and kept respect in Loudon, which was slow to welcome outsiders.

Quinn's obstinacy also caused problems. For instance, whenever he went to Greer's Hardware to buy nails, he drove the staff nuts. Nails were sold in bulk by weight, but Quinn couldn't be bothered to weigh his. He would just scoop them up and plop them on the counter, as if he expected the staff to know the weight by magic. Most of the locals found it amusing. Quinn certainly did, smiling with every handful. The poor staff at Greer's just found it annoying.

This obstinacy could also make it hard to live with Quinn. His wife constantly complained about his cigar ashes getting on everything. Quinn didn't seem to pay much attention and kept right on smoking. Beth's mother does not remember Quinn and his wife ever sleeping in the same bed, and she spent a lot of time with them as an elementary school child. It was ironic that a man so loved in the community struggled in his own marriage, but Quinn could be a hard, stubborn man. It was what made him a great funeral director.

Quinn had one other noteworthy trait that was probably the key to making his marriage work. I learned early in my pastoral training that the most important trait for a funeral director is compassion. A funeral director I met impressed me that funeral homes provide a service. The only way to serve families dealing with the death of a loved is with compassion. All of the funeral directors I have met are gentle and kind, or at least they acted that way. As they walked with families through the steps of planning a funeral, they were sensitive to moments when grief was about to take over and the family needed a break. I've never heard anyone speak more softly than a funeral director on the job, and in the chaos of new grief, that peace is a gift that helps the bereaved make the necessary arrangements. Compassion was a trait that Frank Quinn had in abundance, and he cared for his wife. They went out together, to parties and to dinner. He played cards with her every week, and they certainly cared for each other. They made it work, and stayed married for over fifty years.

While Bush and Quinn continued plans for a small funeral in tiny Cave Creek Primitive Baptist Church, a media frenzy began. A clipping, most likely from a Loudon newspaper, alerted readers that the funeral was only a month away. Headlined "Bush Breazeale Taking No Chances At Funeral," the article references an earlier story in the same paper. Coverage was building with only a few weeks to go. Rather than let the media coverage take its own course, Augustus Summers decided to be proactive. Instead of sitting back and waiting for reporters to come to Bush, he took Bush on a publicity tour of Knoxville.

The press ate it up. They loved taking pictures of hillbilly Bush in the big city, enjoying the sounds and sights of "civilization." When Bush arrived at Hall's Department Store to be fitted for his funeral suit, radio and newspaper reporters were lined up outside. Hall's realized how big this funeral was going to be, and donated the suit. One of the most endearing pictures of Bush is the Knoxville News-Sentinel's photograph of him trying on that suit, looking at himself in the mirror with his long white beard, studying his appearance. I thought Bush looked confused as he tried on the double-breasted, black pinstripe suit and a fedora. His eyebrows were raised, almost as if he

Huggins, 1938

was asking "Who is this guy?" It was a good question. Not only had Bush never owned a suit in his seventy-three years, he had never even worn one before.

After Hall's, Bush went to the Tennessee Theatre, which had opened in 1928. It is on the National Register of Historic Places, a wonderful example of the boom period of movie palaces. Inside were two thousand seats and an interior designed in Spanish style. Outside, a huge, vertical neon sign glowed with the word "Tennessee." Originally, it was a hodgepodge of international design, featuring French chandeliers, Italian terrazzo flooring, and Oriental carpets and drapes. All of these, combined with a Wurlitzer Organ and East Tennessee's first air conditioning unit, gave it an air of opulence. Like many movie palaces, it closed briefly and fell into disrepair, but it was restored and reopened in 2005. The renovations cost thirty million dollars, but it was restored to its place as a regional cultural center.[88] At the theater, Bush told newspaper reporters he had just seen his first "talking picture." He had seen a silent movie before, but never one with sound, even though no silent films had been produced for almost ten years. Bush told the reporters that he enjoyed it, along with his first experience of air-conditioning.

Picture appears courtesy Frank Huggins, grandson of Augustus Summers

Huggins, 1938

Next on the publicity tour was a live interview on radio station WNOX. At the time it was a local AM station, and even though it has changed frequency, call letters and format several times, it was one of

the earliest stations to broadcast in Tennessee.[89] Though I believe the audio from the show has been lost, Bush seems to have had as good a time there as he did everywhere else on the tour. No doubt he told the same stories he had been telling forever, but everywhere he went, he had a fresh audience. Opinions were not clouded by rumors. Bush was able to be himself, and people loved him, and he loved the attention.

Before the press tour, Bush and Quinn both still thought the funeral would be around thirty people. Afterwards, they expected a couple of hundred. The church only held a hundred. So, with only two weeks left before the funeral, Quinn decided to move it onto the lawn. Next to the church stood a giant sycamore tree. He would put the funeral tent there so it would be shaded. A stage had to be built so the people in back would be able to see. Some kind of sound amplification would be needed, which meant a sound system and electricity. Even with such a system, more musicians would be required to ensure that everyone could hear. More funeral programs would need to be printed. The Quinn Funeral Home staff got to work.

As the funeral director, Quinn was the host. It was his job to make everyone as comfortable as they could be. The only relief from the stifling summer heat was hand fans, so at summer funerals, Quinn provided ones that said "Quinn Funeral Home." It was the only advertising he ever did. Because they were cheaper to buy in bulk, he had fifteen hundred of them. He was certain he had more than enough.

The funeral kept growing, and it became obvious that there would be many people attending who did not know Bush. At that time, this was not unusual, even for funerals where the person was dead. Funerals were often great social events. Like today, they were one of the few times large groups of extended family and friends got together. Few people were concerned that the funeral might have a social atmosphere, because they were accustomed to that. They saw this one as a chance to get together for a grand social occasion, and the buzz grew.[90]

One group that did not plan to attend Bush's funeral were the prominent citizens of Loudon. Though Bush's live funeral was all anyone talked about, and though it appeared respectable, it had become something of a circus. Prominent business leaders, such as Col. Bacon, found the funeral beneath them. There was nothing wrong with it, but it was an event for the average person. It was something for the common people to enjoy, but beneath the leaders of the community.

One week before the funeral, it was time to assemble a team to actually conduct it. Singers from all over the area were eager to participate. One group that volunteered was the Friendly Eight Octet from Chattanooga. Under the leadership of Clyde A. Blaylock, they were willing to travel ninety miles to sing for free. The Kingston Quartette, a local group, also volunteered to sing, as did Fred Berry of Berry Funeral Home in Knoxville. While I first thought it odd that the owner of another funeral home would sing, evidently Fred Berry commonly sang at funeral homes besides his own. Moreover, Berry Funeral Home was in Knoxville, after all. Though today the two funeral homes are only a thirty-minute drive apart, back then they were in separate worlds. If anyone had told Quinn or Fred Berry that they were competitors, they would have laughed.

For some reason, A.J. Pelham, the pastor of Cave Creek Primitive Baptist Church, was not chosen to speak. Neither was the pastor of the Missionary Church. Instead of a local minister, Reverend Charles Jackson of Paris, Illinois would speak. Jackson was the former pastor of a church in Rockwood, a modest community on the opposite side of Kingston from Cave Creek. Jackson may have known Bush before the funeral, but I could not find anyone who knew how, nor could I find any record of their relationship. Augustus Summers once lived in Rockwood, so perhaps that was the connection. Frank Anderson shared that some of Bush's relatives had gone to Jackson's church in Rockwood, so that could have been it, too. Jackson's participation was announced only two days before the funeral, but may have been arranged long before then. No one knows. It was a mystery to me why Jackson was asked to speak, and why he agreed to come all the way from Illinois to participate.

Frank Anderson, researched Jackson extensively and discovered that he was a man of prominence. Among Jackson's accomplishments were the creation of the Tennessee Sports Hall of Fame and a Christian football bowl for high school teams. The profits from these two ventures were used to create a home for wayward boys. Jackson's participation added both credibility and mystery to Bush's live funeral.[91]

Jackson added credibility for reasons beyond his accomplishments and his status as a minister. Locals remembered him as a person of strong character. Frank Anderson told me a story about Charles Jackson's son that shows what kind of men the Jacksons were. In 1958, Charles Jackson Jr., nicknamed Stony, went to New York City to appear on the phenomenally popular television quiz show "The $64,000 Question." Such shows were all the rage, providing a ratings bonanza for the stations and captivating the nation. Stony Jackson won several thousand dollars, a year's wages in those days, but was shocked to discover that the shows were rigged based on who would get the best ratings. When Stony returned home to Tennessee and told people that the game shows were rigged, nobody but his father believed him. He had lost; folks thought it was just sour grapes.

Herb Stempel soon blew the whistle on the whole operation, and everyone realized Stony had been telling the truth. Congress investigated, and Stony Jackson was called to testify before a federal grand jury. Rumors swirled that many contestants perjured themselves rather than attack the popular quiz show, but with the support and encouragement of his father, Stony Jackson told the truth. As a result, "The $64,000 Question" was cancelled. The 1994 film "Quiz Show," which tells the story of this quiz show scandal, captures the enormous pressure these contestants were under. Stony Jackson's honesty took a tremendous amount of character, and it shows what kind of men Stony and his father were.

During the final week before the funeral, the service itself was planned. A typical funeral service of the day was mostly hymns. The funeral would open with a couple, a prayer, and then another song or two. Then there might be a eulogy, which was a remembrance by a friend or family member. After that, the minister would read something from the bible and give a sermon. The funeral ended after another hymn or two had been sung. Such was the traditional format of an Appalachian funeral, and what Bush planned, except that he would be alive.[92]

Because he was alive, other events leading up to the typical East Tennessee funeral did not occur.

Normally, women would help prepare the body, which would be washed and then dressed. Men were buried in their best clothes, women in a black shroud. Children were buried wearing white. Pennies were placed over the eyes of the dead, to keep their eyelids closed. None of this was done because Bush wasn't dead. Family and members of the community did gather at the home of the deceased, though. Bush seemed always eager for company.[93]

As other final details were set in the week leading up to the funeral, updates were given daily on the radio and in the newspaper. Reporters, eager for a story, provided readers with daily updates on the preparations Bush, Summers and Quinn were making. Soon, everyone knew that flowers would be provided by three businesses: Baum's of Knoxville, Bowdens of Lenoir City, and the Day-McAmis Co. of Chattanooga. They also knew that the six pall bearers would be Bush's fox hunting friends: John McNabb, Dave Evans, and Walter Smith of Kingston, Sam McNabb (J.Y.'s father), Walter Brooks of Lenoir City, and John "J.W." Grubb of Loudon.[94]

Two days before the funeral, Reverend Jackson visited Bush to discuss his message.[95] Preachers often do this before a funeral. Even if I know the deceased well, I talk to the family. In this unusual case, Jackson had the opportunity to ask Bush what he wanted said, and Bush told him. Bush said that he wanted his name cleared, that he had not lived a good life before he had got religion, but that he had also not done some of the things of which he had been accused. He wanted people to understand and to like him. Those were Bush's goals.[96] With hundreds of people expected, I'm sure Jackson had prepared notes in advance, but it was not until after he sat down with Bush at the cabin that he actually wrote out the sermon.

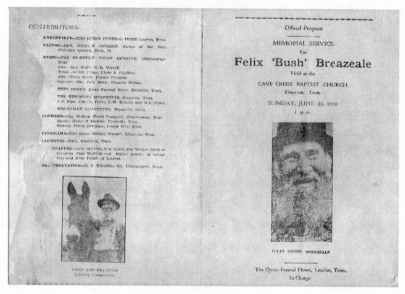

Author, 2010

Finally, it was time to prepare the program. Hundreds were printed. They were simple enough: a letter-sized sheet of paper, folded once to create a booklet with a front, two inside pages, and a back page. The front cover read:

Official Program

MEMORIAL SERVICE

For

Felix 'Bush' Breazeale

Held at the

CAVE CREEK BAPTIST CHURCH

Kingston, TN

SUNDAY, JUNE 26, 1938

2 p.m.

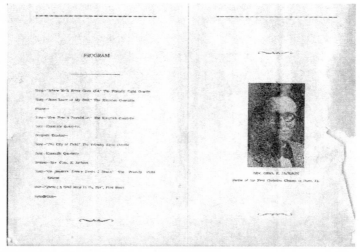

Author, 2010

Below this was a close-up picture of Bush's smiling face. At the bottom was printed:

The Quinn Funeral Home, Loudon, Tenn.

In Charge

The weather was brutally hot as final preparations were made with one day left. Signs pointing folks to the funeral popped up along roads. Visitors started to arrive from out of town in cars, and on buses. One town's bus had a sign on it that read "This Bus to the Breazeale Funeral." A few enterprising locals stocked up on ice cream, hot dogs, and Coca-Cola to sell. That evening, some travelers pitched tents along the road to the church.[97]

On hot nights, many people in Loudon, and other Tennessee towns, slept outside on porches, lawns, and even in the town square if the weather was clear. Beth remembers Granddaddy talking about how the whole town would gather in the town square in Loudon to sleep under the stars. Everyone, from all walks of life, came together for an outdoor slumber party. Born of necessity, it was one of Granddaddy's favorite memories of childhood. Though people often slept outside on hot ones, this time it added to the festive atmosphere. Those who camped close to the church got a good parking spot.

Everywhere, groups of people were gathering, and everywhere they were talking about what would happen the next day. Despite all the newspaper and radio stories, no one knew for sure. Brack Smith and the murder trial still had not been mentioned in any of the news coverage, nor had Bush's bad reputation. Car after car, bus after bus, people came from all around to see Bush's funeral, and they didn't know any of the rumors. In the press, he had been whimsical and funny, and not at all a Boogeyman. No one from outside had any idea why such a warm, friendly man would want to have his funeral while he was still alive. The hills and hollers buzzed with anticipation.

Carloads of early birds, who could not wait for the funeral, drove the three miles from the church to Bush's home in the late evening. Bush greeted them warmly, trotting out Mule to do her tricks, but only for a little while.[98]

"Mule is tired of showing off," Bush said. "Everyone wants to see her cut up a little." Polite people understood that what Bush meant was that it was time for them to go, so they did. Bush went to sleep "listening to the music he loves best in this world: walker hounds driving a red fox hard over the ridges and down through the hollers."[99]

Chapter Seven

Uncle Bush's Live Funeral

It was June 26, 1938. Bush's big day had arrived.

By all accounts, the weather was brutally hot. Normal summer highs in East Tennessee in the 1930's were in the upper eighties, but that day the temperature reached almost one hundred degrees. High humidity made the hot day almost unbearable. At two o'clock, the funeral would take place during the hottest part of the day. In the age before air-conditioning, there was no relief from such heat. When folks could, they passed the afternoons on the coolest part of the house - the front porch - fanning themselves.

On days when they had a social engagement, though, they just had to suffer; the dress code of the day did not make exceptions for the heat. Everyone coming to Bush's funeral wore their "Sunday best." Well to-do women were at least able to wear dresses topped with lace-wrapped hats, adorned with bows or flowers. The dresses were long, though, and most wore girdles underneath. Almost all of the men also wore hats, mostly fedoras, ties, and jackets. A few, those who could afford them, wore suits. Farmers came in the best of whatever they had. Usually this was a long sleeved, cotton shirt and trousers for men, and some type of dress for ladies. Larger hats, the kind worn in the field, were in abundance. It was the only shade many would get on a sweltering day.

That morning, Bush invited twelve friends and family members to join him as he got ready. Bush's home had the feel of a wedding party, and he was constantly making jokes. Given how new he was to the spotlight, it would have been understandable if he had had some butterflies, but on the big day, Bush was not anxious or nervous. After so many years of unwanted isolation, the center of attention was a comfortable place. Bush had finally found the right limelight, and he was ready.

Granddaddy and Quinn arrived early to help Bush prepare. This must have felt normal to them, as part of a funeral director's job is overseeing the physical preparation of the body for the visitation and funeral. This was no different, except that the body was alive and cracking jokes. They arrived in the hearse so they could load the casket in the back. The man who would normally be in the casket would ride in the passenger seat. Granddaddy would drive, while Quinn went ahead to make sure everything was ready at the funeral site.

Finally, it came time to dress in his brand new suit. While everyone else waited in the sitting room, Bush went into his room to dress. He had been in there for a little while when he poked his head out from behind the bedroom door.

"Mr. Quinn," he began in his soft accent, "you have some practice putting on dead men's clothes. I don't know whether you have any with live men, but come on in here."[100] Laughter ensued, and Granddaddy and Quinn went in. Bush needed help with his

BVD underwear. Today, men's underwear covers the groin, and sometimes includes a t-shirt. This underwear, which was typical formal underwear of the day, was a one piece union suit that covered a person's upper thighs, waist, stomach, chest and upper arms. It fit like a modern woman's one-piece bathing suit, only with short sleeves and legs.

"You gonna put on the underwear?" Granddaddy asked.

"I wondered what those were for," Bush answered. Somehow, Granddaddy and Quinn helped Bush get dressed, and soon he came out to show his friends and family his fine suit.

"Well, now, if I'd had these when I was young, I might have married," he said.[101] Instead of the fedora he usually wore, Bush had chosen a straw Italian Boater hat. Flat-topped and flat-brimmed, it had a black ribbon around it.

Author, 2010

"It's the first time I ever seen Bush with a whole suit of clothes on," observed John McNabb, one of the pallbearers.[102]

Waiting outside was a crowd of newspaper reporters and photographers from the Knoxville News-Sentinel, the Knoxville Journal, the Chattanooga Times, the Chattanooga News and Free Press, and the Associated Press.[103] Several neighbors were there, too. Mule kept them entertained as they waited. When Bush finally emerged, he answered questions and had his picture made. Quinn left for the church. Then it was time to load the casket.

The Quinn Funeral Home hearse was typical of the day. It was essentially a longer version of a four-door car, with round headlights sticking out on either side of the engine grille, and running boards the length of both sides. These were wide enough for a person to stand on, and sloped up and over the front tires. The engine compartment was boxy, long and tapered, narrow at the front and widening to meet the passenger compartment. Windows ran all the way around, including where the casket went. With two rows of seats and a spacious back, it held four people and a casket in relative comfort.

Of the pallbearers, only John McNabb was at the house that morning, so the casket was carried out by four employees of Quinn Funeral Home. On the back corner of a newspaper photograph, partially obscured, was Granddaddy. Bush walked behind, in the place normally reserved for immediate family.

Wilson, "Bush Walks Behind His Casket."
Knoxville News Sentinel, Knoxville, TN.

A massive flower arrangement covered almost the entire lid of the casket. It was so tall that it reached to the men's shoulders. Modern caskets are made of metal or thick, heavy wood. With a body in them, six men struggle to carry one. Eight are sometimes necessary. Bush's casket, made of thinner wood and without the body, was easily carried by the four men. Bush got in the passenger seat of the hearse and Granddaddy climbed into the driver's seat. They drove down the one-lane, dirt road, turned right, and stopped at Dogwood School. A crowd followed in their cars.[104]

At Dogwood School, they met the other five pallbearers: Dave Evans, Walter Smith, Sam McNabb,

Walter Brooks, and J.W. Grubb.[105] Bush's friends, Horace Brooks and Ebb Huff, were also there. Huff had driven a reporter past Bush's house on the way to the school and remarked that he had tried to buy Mule from Bush. The closest they got on a price was ten dollars apart, so the deal never happened. Huff remarked that, if sold, Mule "would've been in Georgia making cotton, not in Tennessee getting his picture made."[106]

Quinn told Bush it wouldn't do to get to the church too soon, so he waited at the school. While he waited, the crowd at the school grew. More reporters came. To pass the time, Bush and his friends discussed their favorite topic: fox hunting. According to the News-Sentinel, "had it been later, they may have skipped the funeral and gone hunting." The wait became an impromptu hound memorial. Bush's dogs were the most discussed. Before celebrating Bush's life, he and his Ridgerunner friends celebrated the lives of the closest thing he had to children: his hunting hounds. One, named Yaller Eyes (yellow eyes), was his last. Yaller Eyes had been trained to run off any nearby foxes before Bush let the chickens out to graze. Laughter erupted when they talked about Davy Crockett, named after the Tennessee folk hero who had been born in Greene County, three counties to the northeast. Davy Crockett, the hound, had chased house cats as much as foxes. Bush and his friends guffawed as they told some of the stories of his misadventures. Plenty of stories of other old dogs were told: Dinah, Phil, Trusty, Stonewall, and Founder.[107]

After a lot of fond memories and laughter, it was time for Bush to set out. Granddaddy drove on, Bush in the passenger seat. This time, an even greater crowd followed. In this respect, Bush's funeral was like many today, with the cars of loved ones lined up behind the hearse to make the journey together. With most funerals, this procession takes place from the service to the burial, but in this case, it was from Bush's house to the service. The effect was the same, though: a long line of cars proceeding very slowly. They turned onto Dogwood Road, which became Cave Creek Road and took them around the bend to Cave Creek Primitive Baptist Church. On the dipping, twisting roads, the procession stretched back farther than the eye could see.

Many of those who lived along the procession's path sat on their front porch to watch. Others had pulled chairs out onto their lawns. Rocking on porch chairs, sitting outside on dining room chairs, and lying against fences, people positioned themselves anywhere they could to watch the spectacle of Bush's funeral procession. Houses were far enough apart that it was not a solid wall of spectators. Rather, it resembled the Tour de France as it passes through the French countryside. If you ever get the chance to watch the Tour on television, you will see the riders cycling down empty roads dotted with clusters of spectators watching, cheering and waving from the shade. That's how the crowd along Bush's funeral procession looked. Many of these people had seen Bush plenty of times before, but this was different. They wanted a glimpse of the man of the hour on the way to his much-anticipated funeral. All along the slow, four-mile drive, Bush's funeral procession looked and felt like a sparsely attended parade.

The parade quickly ran into one of the first traffic jams in East Tennessee history. Like Bush, many people in the area still travelled by horse or mule. No one had ever seen that many cars before, and the roads could not handle it. Bush leaned out the window from the passenger seat to gawk.

"Looks like I ain't goin' to get to my own buryin'," he said.[108] By this point, many of those behind the procession had parked and were walking past. Obviously, the hearse gave away who was inside. Many of those who passed stopped, and soon yet another crowd had gathered. Mopping sweat off their faces, they pressed their noses to the windows on all sides of the hearse to get a look at Bush.

Wilson, "Happy Body Looks at Crowd from Hearse." Knoxville News Sentinel, Knoxville, TN.

"He looks like the preacher himself, so dressed up," one woman remarked. Others reached through the open front window to shake Bush's hand and greet him.

"Bush, you're a-gonna be late to your own funeral," someone observed. Bush did not seem bothered by that at all. Instead, he asked for a glass of water.

"We kin just have the buryin' right here," Bush noted dryly. "They can't have it up yonder without me."[109]

While they waited for someone, anyone, to rescue them, a woman thrust a Quinn Funeral Home fan at Bush through the open passenger window. Bush took it, started fanning himself with it, and said to her, "You should get one of these for yourself."

"Autograph, Uncle Bush!" another woman pleaded. "Autograph!" Bush looked over at Granddaddy.

"What do they mean about this autograph?" he asked.

"I think she wants you to sign your name, Bush."

"I'm just too nervous to sign my name," Bush said. "You sign it for me."

So Granddaddy, who could write whereas Bush could not, took the fan. He wrote 'Best Wishes- Uncle Bush' in beautiful script, added an underscore, and handed it back. Another poked through the window. Granddaddy wondered how fans that had been intended for distribution at the church had gotten into the hands of people so far away, but never did find out. He signed that one, and the next, and the next. They kept coming, more and more hurriedly, and he knew he needed to stop before the crowd became too animated, but there was nowhere to go. Despite the blazing heat, they had to roll up the windows to stop the autograph seekers.

"All I could think," Granddaddy told me, "was that I was glad Bush took a bath that spring."

Traffic going to the funeral from the other direction was actually worse. Cars were backed up from the church all the way up to Dixie Highway, the main road into the area. The final three miles of the road to the church turned into a parking lot.[110] Everyone kept their conduct orderly. Not only was no one driving away from Cave Creek, no one driving into Cave Creek tried to drive in the opposite lane. State Police, who had been asked to help with the traffic, did a good job keeping it orderly, though they could not get it moving faster. Rather than dampen people's spirits, the novelty of a traffic jam raised them. This was really going to be something!

As traffic backed up, several farmers seized the moment and started tearing down sections of fencing. Standing on the side of the road, they waved cars through, to park in their pastures. One man, a mill owner named Summers, later mused to Rick Holt that he wished he had known how many were coming that day. If he had, he would have opened more of his pasture, and would have made more than the thirty dollars he pocketed. According to the United States Bureau of Labor and Statistics, the average annual salary in the United States in the 1930's was around fifteen hundred dollars per year. Gas was ten cents a gallon, a loaf of bread was a dime, and a gallon of milk was a quarter. Summers made a week's worth of wages in one morning.

John Cook's pasture - Author, 2010

John Cook made even more. He owned a pasture along the creek bottom and fattened his cows on the thick grass that grew in the rich, fertile soil. That pasture was next door to Cave Creek Missionary Baptist Church, which shared the parking lot with the Primitive Church hosting the funeral. Cook turned his pasture in a parking lot and charged twenty five cents per car, an exorbitant price. Twelve hundred drivers

gladly paid it. For years after, he gleefully told anyone, including Rick Holt, how he made three hundred
dollars that day. It was two months' pay.

Most of those who parked in John Cook's pasture
got out of their cars and walked the short distance to
the funeral without any idea of the history they had
just driven over. Cook's property spread over part of
Brack Smith's old farmstead. Thousands of people
who came to Bush's funeral parked, or walked, on
land owned by the man whose murder had necessi-
tated it. The barn to which Smith was returning when
he was shot had been demolished years before to
build Cave Creek Road, but many of those who came
to the funeral got there by driving right over where it
used to stand. Some locals knew, of course, but even
they did not seem to have much reason to pause. That
day belonged to Bush.

Cave Creek Primitive Baptist Church - Author, 2010

After he had left Bush's cabin, Quinn travelled to the Primitive Church for final preparations. Both it and the Missionary Church were white clapboard, long and narrow with pointed steeples, but the Missionary Church was unbothered, almost forgotten, while the Primitive Church was mobbed. Next to the Primitive Church was the giant sycamore tree that would shade the funeral. When it was last measured in 1979, the tree was eighty-nine feet high and sixteen feet around, making it one of the largest sycamores in Tennessee.[111] Under its low, thick canopy, Frank Quinn's men had erected the tent, the simple word "Quinn" writ large over the front. There was no stage because the tent was not high enough. The frill around the top was six feet off the ground, so anyone outside would not have been able to see anyone taller than that on the inside. There was just a podium and, in front of it, the cloth draped casket stand. Next to the casket stand, a chair waited for Uncle Bush.[112]

Wilson, "Roane County's Greatest Crowd Attends Funeral."
June 30, 1938. Roane County Banner, Kingston, TN

Early in the morning, the small parking lot already overflowed with cars. By noon, it also overflowed with people. On the level grass in front of the tent, the crowd grew and grew until it wrapped around the sides. Flimsy ropes kept folks out, and the only people who crossed them were a few who reached over to pluck a souvenir flower. Once the sides of the tent were packed with people, the crowd filled in behind them, quickly surrounding cars that had been properly parked hours before. The wall of cars blocked the view of new arrivals, but also provided a tempting seat. Quinn asked the owners of these cars to move them, and all but a couple did. That problem was easy to fix.

Virtually everything else about the crowd overwhelmed the Quinn Funeral Home staff. Fifteen hundred hand fans were far too few. Funeral programs, though they had seemed abundant when Quinn had them printed, were rare enough that they became treasured souvenirs. Crowd control was non-existent. Nature was the only restroom. There was no place to sit, and the throng became so tight that it rippled. Strangers stood shoulder to shoulder, front to back, pressed so tightly they had trouble making room to raise their arms. In the stifling summer heat, the buttoned-up mass of bodies became an oven. An hour before the funeral was even scheduled to start, the first person passed out. The smell was unpleasant, to say the least. Those in the back could buy ice cream, sandwiches, hot dogs, and cold Coca Cola. The only relief for those in the middle and front came from the steady, gentle breeze that barely tickled them.

The crowd was massive and difficult to measure. No tickets had been sold, there were no turnstiles, and there was no frame of reference to guess at the number. Thousands and thousands poured in, clogging the empty country roads and fields with their cars and the still country air with their engines and voices. So many abandoned their cars and walked that they seemed to be coming from everywhere. Even the press was stumped as to how many of them there were. None of the newspapers printed a specific attendance figure. They all reported wide ranges. The Roane County Banner said it was between five and fifteen thousand, both the lowest and the highest estimates. The Knoxville News-Sentinel estimated between eight and thirteen thousand. The average guess among the media was ten thousand, but no one knew for sure.

Regardless of how many people came, they definitely came from far and wide. The license plates of fourteen different states were seen. Kentucky, Georgia and North Carolina, the three nearest states, were well represented. So were the distant Tennessee border states of Alabama, Missouri and Arkansas. Even the state of Washington was represented, apparently by distant relatives of Bush.[113] Before the interstate system, when it took the United States Army Transcontinental Convoy sixty two days to drive across the country,[114] people came from all over to see Uncle Bush and his live funeral.

Two celebrities were reportedly there. One was the man who would become the King of Country Music, Roy Acuff, who was just starting his career at the time.[115] Acuff had been working as a musician at local radio station WNOX, on whose airwaves Bush had spoken not long before. Later, he moved to Nashville and performed at the Grand Ole Opry. He eventually received almost every honor a musician could, including a star on the Hollywood Walk of Fame. The other celebrity was Judge Sue K. Hicks,[116] who was the original (but not final) prosecutor in the infamous Scopes Monkey Trial, which took place in the next county over.[117] Hicks would later be the inspiration for the Johnny Cash song "A Boy Named Sue." Both Acuff and Hicks arrived without fanfare, and waited in traffic like everyone else.

The two o'clock start time came and went, and the hearse was nowhere to be seen. Frank Quinn, along with State Highway Patrol officers, set out on foot to find it. They walked up the road, alongside stopped cars, toward Bush's cabin, and found the hearse gridlocked more than a mile away. The Highway Patrol got to work directing traffic. They walked in front of the hearse in the opposite lane, stopping oncoming cars and forcing them to the side so the hearse could pass. Thus, the hearse slowly drove to the funeral in the wrong lane.

At two thirty, the hearse finally arrived at the church. Bush and Granddaddy got out, and the pallbearers assembled behind the hearse to lift the coffin. While they did, Frank Quinn started making his way to the stage. The pallbearers began carrying the coffin to the tent, with Bush following behind. By now, the crowd had fanned out, covering the creek bottom and up onto the ridge behind.[118] People who had been jostling for their spots for hours were not inclined to move, even for Bush, but there was no way around. Bush had to go through the packed crowd to get to the tent.

"Don't shove, don't crowd," Quinn implored over the microphone after fighting his own way to the stage. "Give them room!" Not only did no one listen, the jostling actually grew worse. The crowd began waving back and forth, the tent pitching and heaving as people swayed into the tent's metal poles and ropes. It looked like a school of fish, all moving in unison. The funeral home staff became bouncers, shoving people into each other so the casket could pass, and so Bush could pass behind it.[119]

Finally, at almost three o'clock, an hour after the funeral was supposed to start, the casket reached the

Wilson, title unknown. Knoxville News Sentinel

funeral tent. Four of the pallbearers had been separated from their cargo in the throng. Neither Bush nor
anyone up front knew where they had gone. Bush arrived as two massive floral arrangements were placed
on the casket. First, he warmly greeted all those who
were helping with the funeral. Then, taking off his
hat, he sat down in his chair next to the casket and
asked if anyone had a comb. Faces lit up at this
strange request. Sure enough, someone whipped out
a comb and handed it to him. Instead of combing his
hair, though, Bush combed his beard, probably to re-
lax himself after the harrowing journey. The crowd ate
it up. The mountain man was combing his beard! It
was perfect.[120]

Quinn Funeral Home workers managed to cajole
the crowd into backing off the tent a bit. The people in
front helped, tak-
ing it upon them-
selves to form a
human barrier to
keep those behind
them at bay. This
gave Bush a small
bubble of space.
He sat in his chair,
fanning himself as
f l a s h b u l b s
popped. Photog-
raphers took pic-
ture after picture.
Bush, as he would
during the entire

Wilson, "Roane County's Greatest Crowd Attends
Funeral." Roane County Banner

event, kept his eyes focused above the crowd. The Roane County Banner wrote that "his eyes held something that was not in the faces of the crowd around him," a beautiful calm and serenity.[121] It was as if he was looking at an angel.

Almost everyone was ready for the funeral to start, including Reverend Jackson. The only ones missing were six members of the Friendly Eight Octet from Chattanooga. They were having the same problem as the four pallbearers: they couldn't get to the tent. The two singers who were already present had arrived early, but the other six were still stuck in the horrendous traffic jam. Since the Friendly Eight Octet was to sing the first hymn, everyone waited as the missing members fought through the crowd. Their name proved to be no help; no one cared how friendly they were. With the help of the Quinn Funeral Home staff, they finally made it through and took their seats behind the podium. With them sat the other singers, Reverend Jackson, and Quinn.[122]

It was finally time to start Un-

Wilson, "Principal and Helpers In Funeral That Had No Buryin'." Knoxville News-Sentinel

cle Bush's live funeral. Reverend Jackson stood, took the microphone, and called for silence. Only moments before, the field had been a massive "shove fight," but at the sound of Jackson's voice, it stilled. The light breeze still blew, and the crowd was so quiet that the rustling of Sycamore leaves could be heard. To open the funeral, Reverend Jackson asked the Friendly Eight Octet to come forward and sing "Where We'll Never Grow Old."[123] Written by James C. Moore in 1914, I first heard it sung by Johnny Cash on his posthumous box set "Unearthed." With just Johnny and his guitar, it was a song of longing and hope. Bush's funeral began with these words, sung in rich, full harmony by the octet of four men and four women:

I have heard of a land on a faraway strand,

'Tis a beautiful home of the soul;

Built by Jesus on high, where we never shall die,

'Tis a land where we never grow old.

Refrain:

Never grow old, never grow old,

In a land where we'll never grow old;

Never grow old, never grow old,

In a land where we'll never grow old.

At this point in the song, about halfway through, the loudspeaker stopped working. Frank Quinn had done his best to get a quality sound system, but the size of the crowd had compelled him to turn the volume up as high as it would go, and he blew out the speaker. It had barely lasted a minute. The crowd had overcome even Frank Quinn's meticulous planning.

With a lurch, they surged forward to hear. Ropes creaked and iron strained as the tent rocked, but the human wall around it did its job. The tent stayed up.[124] The song continued:

> In that beautiful home where we'll never more roam,
>
> We shall be in the sweet by and by;
>
> Happy praise to the King through eternity sing,
>
> 'Tis a land where we never shall die.
>
> *Refrain*
>
> When our work here is done and the life-crown is won,
>
> And our troubles and trials are o'er;
>
> All our sorrow will end, and our voices will blend,
>
> With the loved ones who've gone on before.
>
> *Refrain*

During the entire song, Bush kept his eyes on the sky above the crowd, gently waving his fan. He looked at peace, and he soaked up the tune.[125]

Next up should have been the Kingston Quartette, four men who had planned to sing "Jesus, the Lover of My Soul." While many hymns exist with that name, the version they were going to sing was written by Charles Wesley in 1740. It was a long song, with five verses and no refrain. The last verse would have been particularly appropriate:

> Plenteous grace with Thee is found,
>
> Grace to cover all my sin;
>
> Let the healing streams abound;
>
> Make and keep me pure within.

Thou of life the fountain art,

Freely let me take of Thee;

Spring Thou up within my heart;

Rise to all eternity.

Unfortunately, the group had backed out at the last minute. They were in the program, but they never performed this song, nor the one after, "How Firm a Foundation." According to Frank Anderson, they had cancelled at the last minute for religious reasons. Thinking Bush's live funeral bordered on sacrilege, they chose, at the last minute, not to participate. It was the only protest of Bush's live funeral, and it was a silent one.[126]

Reverend Jackson skipped over the Kingston Quartette and led a prayer. Then came another song, this one by the Knoxville Quartette. The name of the hymn was not printed in the program, and I could not discover it. During it, a man and some children started fanning Bush, who accepted graciously. After the singing, murmurs began as Reverend Jackson approached the podium, opening his King James Bible as he walked. It was time for him to read the scripture for the day.[127]

The reading was Psalm Twenty-Three, one of the most popular and well known Bible passages of all time. Most of the funerals I have performed have included this reading. It is a soothing, peaceful proclamation of God's protection and comfort when things are at their worst. Though there were several versions of the Bible that Jackson could have chosen, the King James was the most popular one in East Tennessee back then. Jackson read:

> The Lord is my shepherd, I shall not want.
>
> He maketh me to lie down in green pastures.
>
> He leadeth me beside the still waters.
>
> He restoreth my soul.
>
> He leadeth me in the paths of righteousness for his name's sake.
>
> Yea, though I walk through the valley of the shadow of death, I will fear no evil, for thou art with me.
>
> Thy rod and thy staff, they comfort me.
>
> Thou preparest a table before me in the presence of mine enemies.
>
> Thou anointest my head with oil.
>
> My cup runneth over.
>
> Surely goodness and mercy shall follow me all the days of my life: and I will dwell in the house of the Lord forever.

Jackson read it as loudly as he could, but few could hear him. During the reading, Bush remained serene as the corners of his mouth tilted ever so slightly in a smile. The crowd, though, started showing the strain of the heat and constant jostling. After a particularly strong heave, a few of those in front of the crowd stumbled into the casket. It teetered for a moment. All who could see it held their breath, Jackson's reading momentarily forgotten, but they need not have worried. Frank Quinn knew what he was doing when he assembled the casket stand, and it stayed upright, only slightly askew. Through it all, Bush's face glowed, his narrow eyes sparkling. After the casket settled, he leaned his head back on it as if to say "nothing's going to ruin this day."[128]

The crowd, though, was starting to wonder about that. So far, it had been an unexpectedly normal funeral. Most of the excitement had come from the near disasters the crowd itself had almost induced, and none had come from the stage in front. Brushing his beard was the most exciting thing Bush had done all day. He had not climbed into his coffin, nor had he spoken. The question on everyone's mind, the one that brought so many people, remained unanswered. When Jackson finished his prayer, the crowd once again grew quiet. They waited expectantly for him to tell them why Bush was having his live funeral.

Both the Knoxville News-Sentinel and the Knoxville Journal printed the opening portions of Jackson's sermons. They match very closely. According to the News-Sentinel, Jackson began with these words:

"This is an unusual occasion. It is unusual for a man to shape his own casket with his own hands, and for singers to be called from Knoxville and Chattanooga, and for the great concourse of acquaintances and friends to gather. I hope that you did not come with the idea that this was a fantastic affair; that was not what prompted this man to have it. I submit to you that this is more serious than when the corpse is here, because life is more serious than death. It is interesting to find an individual who finds time to make such plans in the midst of life, looking into the future. This is a funeral occasion that is divested of heartbreaks and heartaches."

According to the Journal, he then added:

"It might be a wholesome thing if everyone could hear his own funeral preached."

While Jackson continued to speak, a woman right next to Bush fainted from heat exhaustion. The crowd parted briefly so she could be carried out, then immediately closed up again. Jackson did not pause, but continued to speak about the importance of a man's life being one of significance. The measure of a man, Jackson preached, is what he has done with his life, in what he has built for himself and those around him.[129]

The sermon was general. Jackson never spoke about Bush directly. Brack Smith never came up, nor so much as a hint of eternal damnation. Jackson focused his moving message on the importance of living right rather than the consequences of doing wrong. He talked about living in a way that made people worthy of the trust God showed in giving life to them. Without directly coming out and saying it, Jackson praised Bush for being a good man who had lived a good life.

Though Jackson's thought process was never recorded, I could see what he had done. He knew that if he mentioned murder, stealing, moonshining or adultery, that would be all anyone remembered, and it wouldn't matter if Bush had done those things or not. Once those words came out, no one would hear anything else. So Jackson didn't mention them. Because Jackson didn't mention any sins, people assumed there were no sins to be mentioned. Jackson gave absolution by omission, and the crowd believed Bush was not just a good man, but a great one.

As Jackson worked his magic, Bush watched the crowd. He smiled the entire time. All of these people, each and every one of them, heard what a good person he was. With each word, he shed his reputation as the Boogeyman. He was someone different now. Instead of being the Boogeyman, he was a great man who had put on an incredibly fun live funeral.[130]

Bush had done it.

By the time Jackson was done speaking, the Boogeyman of Cave Creek was no more.

Most Southern Christian funerals end with an altar call, where non-believers are invited to come forward and commit their lives to Jesus. Jackson skipped that. Instead, the sermon concluded with a reading of Bush's obituary. It was very brief. The next day, the Knoxville News-Sentinel printed a summary:

> "The sketch said he was born June 29, 1864, one of the eight children of D.W. Breazeale and Sarah Littleton Breazeale on Dogwood Road where his home still is, most of his life was spent working on the ridges with a bull tongue plow, and spending all of his life except one year in Roane County. The preacher said that Uncle Bush's mother was the sister of Thomas J. Littleton, father of attorney Martin Littleton and Mrs. Rachel Vanderbilt Morgan of New York City."

It was a suitably short summary for a man who wanted to avoid the details of his life.

After Reverend Jackson's sermon came a hymn Bush had chosen: "On Jordan's Stormy Banks I Stand." One of his favorites, it was sung by the Friendly Eight Octet. Bush sang along, patting in rhythm on his arm.

"I aimed to stand up when they sung it, and make some gestures," he later told the Knoxville Journal, "but it's too crowded, there ain't no room."[131]

Written in the late 1700's by Samuel Stennett, "On Jordan's Stormy Banks I Stand" has been well-loved by Southerners for a long time. In 2005 it was recorded by Christian rock band Jars of Clay for their album Redemption Songs. The upbeat melody and lyrics about looking forward to life in heaven make it one of the cheerier songs I've heard about death. More than any other song from that day, this one fit the mood Bush wanted for his funeral:

> On Jordan's stormy banks I stand,
>
> and cast a wishful eye
>
> to Canaan's fair and happy land,
>
> where my possessions lie.

> *Refrain:*
>
> I am bound for the promised land,
>
> I am bound for the promised land;
>
> oh, who will come and go with me?
>
> I am bound for the promised land.

> O'er all those wide extended plains
>
> shines one eternal day;
>
> there God the Son forever reigns,
>
> and scatters night away.

Refrain

No chilling winds or poisonous breath

can reach that healthful shore;

sickness and sorrow, pain and death,

are felt and feared no more.

Refrain

When I shall reach that happy place,

I'll be forever blest,

for I shall see my Father's face,

and in his bosom rest.

Refrain

After this came the final song, "There's A Gold Mine In the Sky." It was most famously recorded by singer Pat Boone in 1957. Like all of the songs at Bush's funeral, it looked forward to heaven, a beautiful place of peace and serenity.

There's a gold mine in the sky far away.

We will find it, you and I, some sweet day.

There'll be clover just for you down the line.

Where the skies are always blue, pal of mine.

It was sung by Fred Berry. As Berry sang the crowd swayed precipitously. Again the casket was bumped, this time with even greater force. It bounced across the casket stand and almost fell on Bush, who remained too busy enjoying the moment to mind.[132]

Thus ended Bush's live funeral. As Bush stood, the bubble around him was popped by a sea of well-wishers. The human fence was overwhelmed as the crowd tried to get a better look at him.

Bush was a hero, a great man who had lived humbly and put on a fantastic live funeral, and everyone wanted to meet him.

Many of those who had watched the funeral from the side surged in to pat the casket. Others plucked a flower or petal, or several of each, from the flower arrangements. Before long the arrangements were "plucked bare, like chickens." Bush himself took several flowers and passed them out. Men left with pockets decorated with lilies, gladiolas or carnation blooms. Women carried off bouquets wrapped in fern. The four pallbearers who were unable to reach the tent finally pushed through, whereupon Bush greeted them with a big smile and a handshake. As the crowd broke up, the vendors were mobbed. Soon all the ice cream and Coca Cola were gone. Thirsty customers drank right in front of the vendors, fanning themselves as they chugged. The ten women who had fainted during the funeral had all been quickly revived, and their friends and families now stood around them as they gathered their strength. Lige

Freels, a seventy-year-old man from nearby Bethel Valley, was one of the first to leave. Unfortunately, it was because he had suffered a stroke during the funeral and was taken to Knoxville for treatment.[133]

Wilson, "Funeral Crowd Is So Dense 10 Faint."
Knoxville News-Sentinel

As the crowd began to break up, many of those who had been stuck in the back came forward to get their first good look at Bush. Funeral programs were thrust out for him to sign. With no gracious way to get out of it, Bush made his 'X' on them. His hands soon began shaking with palsy, so he could sign only a few. Flashbulbs popped and popped. Several of the women who had fainted came forward to meet him, and he greeted them especially warmly. He thanked them for coming and tried to cheer them up.

"This will be my only funeral," Bush told the knot of admirers, "and I'm mighty well pleased with it. When I die, there won't be another one."

Instead of hiding their children, women brought them forward. Rather than shutting them away, mothers held them out for Bush to touch. Other parents lifted their children above the crowd so they could see him. They knew this was a day that would never be forgotten. Their children would tell their children about how they had been there, about how they had seen, and perhaps even met, the famous Bush Breazeale on the day of his incredible live funeral.

Two of Bush's great nieces came forward, Mrs. Mary Kate Breazeale, who had kept Bush's father during his last days, and Mrs. Walter Crow. They invited him to join them for dinner. Bush shook his head. Mule was waiting at home.[134]

"If you'll come on home with me, we'll cook and eat," he told them. "I'm still looking for my dinner."[135]

Reverend Jackson also gave interviews. He told the Knoxville Journal, "If a lot of these roughnecks out there had to face the music before they pass out, it would improve their way of living. This may mark the day of a new era in funerals." Even if it did not, it certainly marked a new era in Bush's life.

Bush stayed to greet as many people as he could. The Journal estimated that after the funeral he personally greeted a thousand people. Every person whose hand he shook was given that same warm smile. Every program shoved in his face, though his hand was weary and he could no longer sign them, was a precious gift. Out in the sun on a brutally hot and humid day, wearing a black suit, surrounded by strangers who pressed in from all sides, Uncle Bush drank every last drop from his cup of redemption.

A reporter finally asked Bush why he wanted to have this live funeral. Hours before, it had been the question on everyone's mind.

"Just like to know what the preacher would say about me, I guess," was Bush's answer.[136] That was good enough. No one seemed to care anymore.

As the sun began to set, the crowd thinned. Only Bush and a few reporters remained. Soft drink vendors collected their empties. Cars tried to drive away, but traffic was actually worse leaving. For five hours, cars crept along the back roads to the highways. Finally, almost everyone had gone from the church. Bush surveyed the scene. The tent had been taken down. The casket had been loaded into the car. The crowd was gone. The funeral was over.

"How do you think it went?" Augustus Summers asked.

"A complete success," Bush pronounced. Summers wrote in the Roane County Banner that this was because:

> The sermon was the finest he had ever heard and he was well-pleased with all the "doin's and goin's on," although he said he never intended for his funeral to be "such a big stir off." He had in mind to have a quiet affair, he said, until the newspapers got "aholt of it" and let everybody know about it.[137]

Bush and the casket went home to Mule, very late for dinner. His pallbearers went with him. Back at Bush's house, they ate and laughed as they shared their favorite moments from the day. They did not stay very long, though.[138] It had been a day unlike any other. Bush went to bed that night tired, and happy. He was certain that his slate had been wiped clean, and that he could spend the rest of his days in peace.

Chapter Eight

The Hero of Cave Creek

Bush's live funeral had been on a Sunday, the traditional day of rest. It was the only day on which farmers did not work. The next day, Monday, he woke up and got back to work. The garden and truck patch needed tending, the livestock needed food and care, and there was no one to do it for him. Bush didn't seem to mind. He had gotten what he wanted. The next time someone whispered when he walked by, it wouldn't be a whisper of accusation, but of praise and admiration. Bush and Mule worked as they did every day, but there was a new bounce in Bush's step. After fifty years in a prison without walls, he was a free man.

While Bush worked, residents of Knoxville and other nearby towns were waking up and getting their morning newspapers. As they drank their morning coffee and ate their country ham biscuits, they read the coverage of Bush's live funeral with amazement. Not only was Bush's funeral the lead story, but both Knoxville newspapers, The News-Sentinel and The Knoxville Journal, devoted three entire pages to it. Each had over a dozen pictures. There was a panoramic crowd shot, and one of a thirsty couple sharing a Coca-Cola. There was a picture of a line of stopped cars, another of a sign pointing to the funeral, and one of Reverend Jackson.

The best pictures, though, were of Bush himself. One is iconic, taken on the way to the funeral and printed on the front page of The Knoxville News-Sentinel. Bush is squinting, his searching eyes above a hint of a grin.[139] Another shows Bush in his "everyday clothes," beaming a huge smile.[140] In every picture, Bush glowed. He glowed as he greeted the crowd, shook hands, and stood at his house after the funeral. It was hard for me to imagine someone looking more happily serene than Bush did in the newspapers after his funeral, and East Tennesseans eagerly read about this incredible event.

One entire article in The Knoxville Journal was devoted to the reactions of those who were there. It was titled "Crowd Lauds Funeral Idea," and it was written by Leslie Hart.

"I just wanted to see what it looked like," J.M. Cook told Hart. Cook was not John Cook who owned the field next to the church, but he lived nearby. He had made $30 parking cars in his distant pasture. Like those who came from much farther away, he was just curious to see what a live funeral looked like.[141]

"It appeals to me for the people to have a little recreation," said J.W. Grubb, one of Bush's pallbearers. "Bush is an old timer. They don't raise 'em like him anymore."[142]

"It will pleasure a lot and hurt none," an anonymous friend of Bush added. Several of those who had gathered at Dogwood School agreed that it was "all right" for Bush to have his funeral if he wanted it.[143]

J.E. Humble had driven down to the funeral from Jamestown, Kentucky. Today, that is a three-hour drive, so in 1938, it was likely at least twice that. "I don't want to hear my funeral until I'm laid out," he told the Knoxville Journal. "Looks foolish to me, but I came all the way down here and I'm not sorry."[144]

"A man likes to hear good things about himself while living," Charles Limburg, 50, of Loudon told the Journal. "Don't believe, though, I want to hear my funeral preached."[145]

"No indeed," said eighteen-year-old Elizabeth Nichols of Loudon, when asked if she would want to hear her funeral preached. "It's all right for others, but leave me out."[146]

"No, I don't want to hear my funeral," answered M.L. Bilbrey, a 77 year old farmer from South Harriman. "I'll get to it soon enough. I'm just about past thinking about this thing. I guess it's all right though."[147]

Mrs. Porter McCown of nearby Lenoir City said she didn't "know whether it was right or wrong." But she, too, knew a living funeral wasn't for her.[148]

Those interviewed agreed that Bush's live funeral was one of the most interesting things they had seen. The Associated Press and United Press International agreed, and sent the story to newspapers across the country, many of which ran it. Three days after the funeral, Bush turned seventy four, and the story had actually gotten bigger.

Invitations started arriving to appear at local events. Despite the massive crowd, most of the people in the area had not been to the funeral. They had laughed at his quotes, been moved by his smile, and now they wanted to meet the "live corpse." Bush's first celebrity guest appearance was at a Fourth of July celebration in Harriman, in northwest Roane County. Only six days after his funeral, this man, who had been shunned for fifty years, was throwing out the first pitch at a baseball game between local teams Harriman and Loudon. He did so in a Harriman team uniform, probably his first time wearing a sports uniform. The advertisement poster read:

LIVING CORPSE

And his homemade coffin

FELIX 'BUSH' BREAZEAL (sic)

The only person to ever hear his own funeral.

HARRIMAN- JULY 4th

In Person - All Day - Free

Talk and shake hands with Roane County's

Most publicized citizen

Mule was on hand as well, and this time the crowd was well controlled. Person after person stood calmly in line for the chance to meet Bush. When their turn came, he shook their hand, talked with them, and got his picture made with them. It was a great day, and other celebrity invitations followed. I would love to have seen Mule sharing the spotlight as a celebrity base runner at Knoxville Smokies minor league baseball games.

Two days after the funeral, Bush was contacted about an appearance on "Ripley's Believe It or Not!" radio program in New York City. Robert Ripley had begun the "Believe It or Not!" franchise as a panel comic in the New York Globe in 1918. Through diligent research, Ripley discovered the 'strange, bizarre and unexpected' and shared these facts with eager readers. At its peak in 1932, daily readership of the comic was eighty million people, about eighty percent of the United States population. In 1930, Ripley began a weekly or biweekly radio program. Varying in length from fifteen to thirty minutes, Ripley's program changed names several times but managed to run until 1948. It was an American institution, and several Ripley's Museums still exist.

Ripley was onto the story early. A Ripley's office memo dated June 28, 1938, two days after Bush's funeral, contained a report of the event for the radio department. It was signed by an investigator named "J.L.S." On the top of the typed memo are the handwritten words "Wedn. Post Bran," referring to the day of the week Bush would be on the program and the sponsor for that day, Post Bran. Below this is written the date, July 26, 1938, which is the date that Bush appeared on the "Ripley's Believe It or Not!" radio program. In the upper right hand corner are written the words "Can Get." Ripley's investigator J.L.S., whoever he was, was at the funeral, and had gotten a preliminary agreement from Bush to be on the radio program one month later.

Then things got interesting.

A telegram dated the same day, June 28, to Bush from Don McClure of Ripley's radio extended a formal invitation to appear. The tone of McClure's telegram conveys a sense of urgency, but he had had to send it to Harriman, because that was the nearest telegraph office. He must have been flummoxed when he received this reply from the Western Union facility where he sent the telegram:

> WE HAVE RECEIVED WORD FROM OUR OFFICE IN HARRIMAN TENN THAT UNCLE FELIX BREAZEALE KINGSTON TENN LIVES ELEVEN MILES OUT ON RURAL FREE DELIVERY ROUTE #2 AND HAS NO PHONE STOP WE MAILED A COPY OF THE MESSAGE WHICH SHOULD REACH HIM TOMORROW MORNING.

McClure required "assurance that [Bush] will not accept any other offer without giving Ripley first chance." Bush gave it, and later that same day, McClure sent another telegram with their first offer, an all-expenses-paid trip to New York and an appearance fee. When Bush's reply arrived at McClure's desk two days later, it was signed by "W. A. Baker, Business Manager." Just a few weeks before, Bush had been a desperate hermit. Now he was such a celebrity that he had a business manager.

Bush accepted their offer and his appearance on Ripley's was scheduled for July 28, 1938, one month and two days after the funeral. Ripley's would pay for train fare and a four-night hotel stay for two, plus a one-hundred dollar appearance fee. At least, that was Bush's understanding. But when the final contract was sent out, six days before his appearance, it read that Bush would receive "the usual fee." No amount was given. It just said "the usual fee." McClure's vagueness made Bush uneasy. When Baker tried to get McClure to clarify, McClure said they would pay fifty dollars. Baker replied that Bush "had been advised that the fee was one hundred dollars." McClure's response was something to make an Enron executive proud.

INFORMATION ON USUAL FEE ERRONEOUS BUDGET DOES NOT PERMIT IN AS MUCH AS WE MUST PAY TWO ROUND TRIP PASSAGES AND EXPENSES IN NEW YORK. PLEASE SIGN CONTRACT AND RETURN. ALL ARRANGE-MENTS HAVE BEEN SET BY SOUTHERN RAILROAD IN KINGSTON GOOD WISHES

The fee amount was not "erroneous." Ripley's was, in fact, reneging on their earlier deal. Internal documents show that they made the offer of one hundred dollars, and then on the same piece of paper, after the telegram had been sent, they hand-calculated the total cost. When they did, they found out that a one-hundred dollar appearance fee pushed the contract over their budget. They kept Bush on the hook, thinking it would be a hundred dollars; then, with less than a week to go, they dropped their offer. I expect they thought that Bush was committed and would not back out despite the decreased offer. Adding "Good wishes" was the perfect touch of irony.

Bush and Baker must have expected Ripley's to pull something like this, because it turns out that they actually set Ripley's up; the reason McClure required "assurance that Bush would not accept another offer" was because they had dropped hints to Ripley's that there were offers from other radio programs. No record of such offers exists. Perhaps they were real, or perhaps they were a negotiating tactic. Regardless, Bush played hardball and dictated the following telegram:

> SORRY NO CAN DO STOP UNCLE FELIX CONCERNED THAT HOTEL WILL BECOME ERRONEOUS ASSUMPTION ONCE IN NY. NOW CONSIDERING OTHER OFFERS. BELIEVE IT OR NOT.

McClure gave in. Bush made the trip to New York City and appeared on Ripley's Believe It or Not! on July 26th, 1938. His appearance fee was one hundred dollars. It was more money than he had ever had.

For ten years, I tried to find a recording of the interview. The first place I looked was the "Ripley's Believe It or Not!" archives, but their copy had vanished. They claimed to have copies of every radio program, but their copy of that show had gone missing. I asked everyone I met, and while a few people remembered hearing the interview, no one had a copy. Until

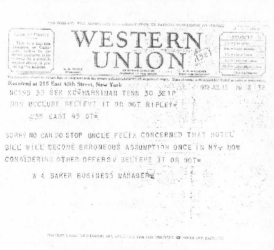

Breazeale, Mick. Date unknown

one day, out of the blue, Uncle Steve called.

Steve had found a website with a lot of information about Uncle Bush. It had pictures, newspaper articles, even court documents. The website was the "Clan Breazeale" website I mentioned in a previous chapter, and it belonged to Mick Breazeale. It not only contained all the Ripley's correspondence on the previous pages, but it also had a recording of Bush's Ripley's interview.

Mick was in his mid-sixties, short and stout, with glasses and pure white hair that could have used a bit of thickening on top. Born and raised near Pascagoula, Mississippi, his accent had faded slightly during the time he spent living in New Jersey and Atlanta. A Bob Dylan aficionado, Mick was a former chiropractor and retired chiropractic teacher. To keep himself busy in retirement, he worked in a veterinary clinic. Mick was a true southern storyteller. When he talked about Bush, he spoke with passion, leaning in and waving his hands for emphasis. There was a special place in his heart for Uncle Bush.

"I heard about it at family reunions," he told me. "My grandpa, his oldest son, and several others took off from Mississippi and drove to Tennessee to meet Bush and Mule." Mick got his passion for genealogy from that same grandfather. At a family reunion, he became inspired to keep the stories of the past alive by starting the Clan Breazeale website. He soon tried to discover his direct connection to Uncle Bush, eventually figuring out that he was descended from Henry Breazeale's second brother, Elisha Bushaloo, who settled in Noxapter, Mississippi, which is pronounced nox-UH-pater and is a little east of the middle of the state.

Mick's investigation into the Bush story began in 2003, when his brother, Steve, called. They had heard the rumors about Bush for years. On a lark, his brother wanted to drive up to Roane County and see what they could find. Steve drove from Mississippi to Atlanta and together they road tripped three hours up I-75 to Kingston. They ended up at the Roane County Heritage Commission, the same folks who had nothing to say to me and welcomed Uncle Steve with open arms. Mick and his brother had a delightful time there. The folks from the Historical Commission were even more helpful to Mick than they had been to Uncle Steve, sharing a thick folder full of information.

"Maybe we just met somebody who was new," I wondered.

"Could be," Mick agreed. "Then again, I'm family, and that might have had something to do with it."

It could have been that, too.

Whatever the reason, the file folders they presented to Mick were stuffed with newspaper clippings, telegrams, and memorabilia. Buried in them was a compact disc. Robert Bailey of the Roane County Heritage Commission happily burned Mick a copy. When Mick played it, he found it was a recording of the entire "Ripley's Believe It or Not!" episode on which Uncle Bush appeared. Mick posted it on the

Clan Breazeale website, and I was able to visit the site and listen.[149]

The quality was lousy in places, and I had to turn up the volume. I strained to hear the voices. Then what sounded like a dot matrix printer leapt out of the speaker and smacked my eardrum. I had no idea what it was, but it sawed away at twice the volume of anything else. The sound was terribly frustrating, but between bursts, I heard Robert Ripley asking questions and Bush answering.

What struck me immediately was how much Bush's voice sounded like Granddaddy. Both spoke in a distinctive East Tennessee accent. I've noticed that in movies set in the South, most actors have tried for "Deep South." In the Deep South, the letter "R" is smoothed over by what is called a "soft R." In East Tennessee, and most of Appalachia, the "R" is pronounced rather than smoothed over. There is also a strong twang in East Tennessee. A lot of people there sound like they should be playing bluegrass music, which is appropriate since bluegrass is quite popular there. The most easily accessible example of an East Tennessee accent that I have found is Dolly Parton. She is from Sevierville, Tennessee, and her accent and expressions come straight from the mountains.

Bush and Granddaddy were born fifty years and eleven miles apart. They sounded as if they were next door neighbors. Not only were their accents alike, but their volume, sentence structure and cadence matched, too. Both spoke softly, in gentle voices that were pleasing to the ear, but would not carry in an open space. Both often started sentences with the word "well." In fact, seven of the fourteen sentences Bush speaks in the Ripley's recording begin with the word "well." When Ripley asked Bush to tell him about the funeral, he answered, "Well…it was a Sunday in June…" Later Ripley asked Bush how smart Mule was, and he answered "Well…it's got more sense than the majority of people has." Granddaddy and Bush also both spoke with the lilt of the storyteller. They knew when to talk faster or slower to draw the listener into the story, and how to arrange words in such an order as to emphasize their intended effect, be it humor or sadness.

Mick transcribed the whole interview. He was gracious enough to share his transcription. The recording began with an ad for Post Bran.

> Yes sir! Life is swell, when you keep well. And, say what a really swell cereal Post Bran Flakes are. So crunchy, and what a wonderful nut-like flavor. And then, those extra benefits. The benefits of bran so many of you may need to help you keep fit, naturally. So, why don't you join the millions who enjoy Post Bran Flakes every day, for their delicious flavor, for their extra benefits. Yes, life is swell when you keep well.

As I listened, I kept waiting for an Ovaltine ad, and for Ralphie from "A Christmas Story" to come on and say "A crummy commercial?!" But no, it was delightfully real.

After the advertisement, Ripley shared the little known fact that it was illegal to dream in Yemen. I had no idea that was the case back then, nor do I know if that ever changed. Heck, I didn't even know Yemen was a country in 1938.

A musical interlude came next, and then Ripley segued into Bush's story.

Ripley: Tonight...I have for you several amazing Believe It or Nots. (pause) Usually, uh, everyone thinks of a funeral as one of the saddest and most solemn of all occasions. But there is one man alive today who looks back at his own funeral as the most joyous event of his life.

Announcer: Well, Bob, I'll bet poor (name unintelligible) is sorry he's on vacation yet. He's not here to hear about that one. But how can a man look back on his funeral and consider it a joyous occasion?

Ripley: Well, Dan, he's standing beside me right now. He is 74 years old. He has come here from Kingston, Tennessee. May I now present Felix Bush Breazeale, known as Uncle Bush. Uncle Bush, will you tell us about this funeral of yours?

Uncle Bush: Well...it was a Sunday in June..."

The end of Bush's answer was lost to static, but the next six minutes were the longest collection of his authentic words I had ever found. Bush did not sound anxious or nervous. He was on one of the biggest stages in the country and he sounded at home. His voice light and lively, Bush joked and told stories and completely charmed me. My favorite exchange:

Ripley: Say, I also understand that you were a half-hour late to your own funeral. Is that true?

Uncle Bush: Yes, half-hour late. They blockaded the road... the people...wantin' me to sign autographs...so we was a half-hour late a-gettin' to the top of the hill where the funeral was to be held.

Ripley: 'Cause you had to stop and sign autographs. Sounds like Hollywood...but tell me, uh, tell me Uncle Bush, uh, just what did you like best about your own funeral?

Uncle Bush: Well sir, the best I liked about it, they didn't bury me after the funeral was over.

A little while later, Ripley flat out asked Bush why he had the funeral.

Ripley: Uh, tell me, Uncle Bush, uh, how did you get the idea of having your funeral before you died?

Uncle Bush: Well, I'll tell ya. I've heared so many funerals preached after a man's dead, you hear so many tales told that weren't so, that I just wanted to hear mine before I died so, if they made any mistake, I could get right up and correct it. (laughter from audience).

Ripley (laughing): Well, Uncle Bush, how about your own funeral, did you have to get up out of that…out of that coffin and correct the preacher?

Uncle Bush: No, sir. He went straight and true.

It's the most direct quote from Bush about why he wanted the funeral.

Bush's goodness had been proclaimed again, only this time it wasn't a mere ten thousand listening. During those six minutes on "Ripley's Believe It or Not!", millions listened, giving him a greater dose of the redemption he sought and a hero status he never expected. For fifty years, Bush had been a Boogeyman. Now he was a beloved national celebrity. Next to the funeral itself, I believe this interview was the highlight of Bush's life.

As Bush was leaving his interview, Robert Ripley gave him his autograph. When Bush returned to Tennessee, he was not sure what to do with it.

"I don't want this thing," he told Granddaddy. "I don't have any reason to keep it. You want it?"

"Well, I'd sure like to have it," Granddaddy said. Beth's Uncle Larry showed it to me.

> To - Uncle Bush
>
> All the best!
>
> Ripley
>
> "Believe it or Not!"

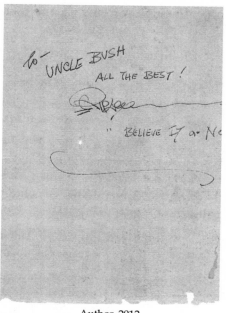

Author, 2012

The Ripley's interview was the high water mark of Bush's fame. For two months that summer, appearance and interview requests poured in, but nothing would ever match that radio interview. Because of it, fan mail came from across the country and around the world. One surprising letter came from a girl in Nazi Germany. Every piece was a balm, and with each one, the wounds of the past faded further away.

Bush dictated answers to as many letters as he could, and graciously welcomed those who stopped by for a visit. One of those summer visitors was Mick Breazeale's aunt, Clara Childress, though her name was Breazeale then. Only twelve at the time of the funeral, she rode with Mick's grandfather on the trip Mick told me about. Mick's grandfather had read about Bush's funeral in the newspaper and wanted to meet him, so one stifling August day he drove his

Willis Knight car from Ethel, Mississippi, to Bush's house, and back again. Three-hundred and fifty miles away as the crow flies, driving there and back would today take perhaps fourteen or fifteen hours. I'm not sure how they made it in only a day back then, but they did. Packed in the car were Clara, her father, her fourteen-year-old sister, Jewel, her brother, Everett, and his wife, Grace. There was no way to call ahead and let Bush know they were coming, and they didn't want to wait long enough for a letter to arrive, so they just got in the car and went.

Fortunately, Bush was home when they arrived. He came out onto the porch and down the steps as everyone piled out. Despite having no idea they were coming, he welcomed them warmly. After introductions, he invited everyone in for coffee. As they entered the house, they noticed a woman around Bush's age. Bush introduced her as his sister, who had come over to help with the "womanly duties" around the house. After some polite conversation, he invited them to the barn across the dirt road. There they met Mule, who showed off a few of her tricks. Set off to one corner was the coffin. Once they were back in the house, Bush poured some more coffee and they visited some more. Soon, Clara and her family were on their way back to Mississippi. More than anything else, Clara remembered how tired and miserable she was during that return trip. Meeting a living legend had been nice though.[150]

As the weather cooled and the leaves started to turn, visitors and fan mail slowed. The requests for interviews and appearances slowed and then stopped. Over the next few years, there was the occasional visitor, but they were few and far between. Bush and his small circle of family and friends had time to reflect on his whirlwind funeral. As they did, second thoughts began to emerge.

"The story I was told," Frank Anderson said, "and I don't mean to offend anybody, but the story I was told was that Bush never got a nickel for any of that, but a lot of people made money off Bush." Obviously, the Ripley's telegrams show that Bush did receive some money. But the feeling among some of the family was that others did better, sometimes much better. John Cook rented parking spaces in his pasture, Augustus Summers sold newspapers, and W.A. Baker, Bush's manager, undoubtedly took a cut of each appearance fee. Fred Berry, Baum's Florist, Halls Department Store, and Quinn Funeral Home all got free advertising. Even the people selling Coca Cola in the parking lot made money, and during the Great Depression, every penny was precious. They were precious to Bush, too, but he never saw most of the money made off of his live funeral. Being famous and being wealthy, I've learned, are not the same thing.

"The story was told with some bitterness," said Anderson. It wasn't that Bush ever regretted his funeral, but he wished he had done more to monetize it and, perhaps, wished also that others had not done so well. Still, it remained the highlight of his life, and he went out of his way to revisit his beloved celebrity. When he travelled to Knoxville, he visited the News-Sentinel offices. He dropped in, like an old friend, to thank reporters and staff for their coverage and for graciously passing on every piece of fan mail sent to him care of their office. On each visit, he relived his glorious day. It was a story he never tired of telling.

Just before the funeral, Bush had developed a palsy that made his hands shake. For a time after the funeral, the palsy was manageable, but he was still a man who lived by himself. Certain jobs were "women's work," and he had no women in the house. Family would come by and help, but he still had to cook and clean. According to Frank Anderson, Bush found this humiliating. As the palsy got worse over the next few years, Bush's fine motor skills deteriorated. Even if he wanted to cook and clean for himself, he reached a point, a few years after the funeral, where he simply could not take care of himself anymore.[151]

"Plus he had trouble with his neighbors," said Frank Anderson. "It was wintertime and when Bush would go to church... or to visit friends or family in the community, someone would break into his house and steal his quilts, which he used to keep himself warm." This happened several times; his quilts just disappeared. When Bush shared this with his niece, Mary Kate Breazeale, and her husband, Burt, along with how he struggled to tend the farm and bring in firewood, they invited him to come live with them. At first he turned them down. Eventually, though, he was forced to accept. According to Frank Anderson, Bush stayed "...in a little half bed in one corner of their bedroom." Then, one day in January of 1943, Mary Kate and Bert came home to find Bush lying still on the floor. He had had a stroke.[152]

Uncle Bush had a second stroke and died in Mary Kate Breazeale's home at 7:30 p.m. on February 9, 1943. It was five years after his funeral, and he was seventy-eight. Though he left behind no children or spouse, he died with family all around him. Both the Knoxville Journal and News-Sentinel ran small articles, but neither mentioned a cause of death. Until the latter half of the twentieth century, it was normal for people to just die at home, of what was commonly called "natural causes." It was not until the 1950's that people began dying in hospitals and nursing homes.[153]

Quinn Funeral Home handled Bush's burial, scheduled for four days later. As Bush had insisted, there would be no second funeral, just a simple burial. Also as he insisted, his visitation was only one hour long. That was all the time friends and family had to come by the funeral home and pay their last respects. Normally, the deceased were laid out for three days. According to Rick Holt, this tradition, like so many others, emerged out of a practical necessity. In this case, the need was to be sure that the person was actually dead. Rick told me that, in the early frontier days, when medicine was rudimentary, checking for a pulse or breathing was more art than science. There were many times when people thought dead were not. Rick said that one of the biggest fears held by people in East Tennessee was of being buried alive, so burials were delayed as long as possible. After three days, and numerous attempts to 'revive' the person, they would be deemed truly dead and fit for burial. As medicine improved and death became easier to diagnose, the three-day waiting period persisted because that was just the way it was traditionally done.

Visitations also usually took place at home, with the rest of the family still living there. Sleeping in a house with a dead relative may sound creepy, but it was a respectful way to honor him or her with your grief, and considered completely normal. It was exceptional that Bush had a visitation at the funeral home, and even more so that it was limited to an hour. He wanted as little fuss as possible, and got what he wanted.

Bush was buried on Sunday, February 13, at 2:00 p.m. in Cave Creek Cemetery. While Bush's live funeral had been on the hottest day of the year in 1938, his burial was on what would turn out to be the coldest day of 1943. His grave was up the hill, within sight of where his famous funeral had been held. Several rows further uphill lay the forgotten grave of Brack Smith. Next to Smith lay his widow, who had been buried next to him even though she had remarried.

According to Granddaddy, between six and ten people attended, including Frank Quinn, Bush's pallbearers, and an unknown minister. Only a few words were spoken. For Bush, that was the point; everything he wanted said had been said at his funeral. He was buried in his famous handmade walnut coffin. Bush lived poor and he died poor, unable to afford a headstone, with no immediate family to buy one for him. A sheet metal marker, eight inches long and four inches wide, was placed on a stake over his grave.

The only writing on the marker was the grave number.

Chapter Nine

The End of an Era

Bush died on February 9, 1943. Though no one knew it at the time, it was a momentous week in United States history. During that week, the German Sixth Army at Stalingrad surrendered, and the Japanese army retreated from the island of Guadalcanal. Stalingrad is considered one of the turning points of World War II in Europe,[154] while Guadalcanal is seen as one of the turning points of World War II in the Pacific.[155] More than either of these, though, another event related to the war would profoundly impact East Tennessee. A week before Bush died, on February 2, 1943, ground was broken on what would become Oak Ridge National Laboratory. Located in Oak Ridge, Tennessee, the laboratory was built less than thirty miles from Loudon. This top secret research center was part of the Manhattan Project, and was critical in building the first atomic bomb.[156] Oak Ridge was the start of many changes that swept through East Tennessee after Bush died.

The foundations of Oak Ridge, and those sweeping changes, had been laid the decade before, in the 1930's, during the Great Depression. Though the Great Depression was difficult in East Tennessee, it was not as devastating as in other places because the economy was already bad.[157] Things did get worse, but only a little. More than the depression itself, how the nation came out of it changed East Tennessee.

To help the nation recover from the Great Depression, President Franklin D. Roosevelt signed the New Deal in 1933. Joblessness actually peaked that year, even though the depression had begun in 1929.[158] One of the first New Deal projects was the Tennessee Valley Authority (TVA). Roosevelt created "a corporation clothed with the power of government but possessed of the flexibility and initiative of a private enterprise."[159] TVA's mandate was to create jobs by building and maintaining hydroelectric dams in the Tennessee River Valley. Their development objectives were "to boost electricity, and for electricity to boost everything else."[160]

It worked. Not only did TVA create jobs, but electricity became cheaper and more available to people and businesses. At the dawn of the twentieth century, the South actually led the nation in electric generation, but it was limited. Richmond, Atlanta, Montgomery and Nashville were all electrified before 1890. In 1902, the South had eleven percent of the nation's urban population but eighteen percent of the municipally owned power stations. The problem was that only the towns and cities had electricity. TVA made electricity available to everyone, cheaply. Not only were poor country farmers able to have it, but the low cost of electricity gave businesses in the South a competitive edge.[161]

The flood controls on TVA dams also had broad impact. Farming improved because water levels could be controlled. Mosquito breeding sites were also reduced, which aided in the elimination of malaria.[162] Today, malaria is found mostly in the third world. In

Africa in 2013, a child died every minute from malaria. But malaria was endemic to most of the United States east of the Rocky Mountains, and during Bush's life, malaria was a serious problem. The flood controls of TVA, along with insecticide application, led to the disease being eradicated from the United States by 1952.[163] The lakes created by TVA dams also became available for recreation, and the land around them became valuable waterfront property. Because of TVA, life in East Tennessee was better at the end of the 1930's than it was at the beginning, but TVA was only the start.

Cheap electricity was one of the reasons Oak Ridge National Laboratory was built where it was. The town of Oak Ridge sprang up seemingly overnight. In just a few months of 1943, one hundred and fifty laboratory buildings were built on top of old farmland. The population of Oak Ridge grew from three thousand in 1942 to seventy five thousand in 1945.[164] Oak Ridge brought some of the smartest, most educated people in the world to East Tennessee. Beth's friend, Stephen Damos, was pastor of a church in Oak Ridge. He told us that when the church was founded, three quarters of the families in it had a member with a PhD. They were smart, well paid, and they liked their new home. Many stayed after they were finished working at Oak Ridge, bringing the first large influx of new people into East Tennessee in a long time.

While new people were coming, longtime residents were coming back with new perspective. World War II took men and families all over the country.

Mimi and Granddaddy were raising two young children, Uncle Larry, who had been born just after Bush's live funeral in 1939, and Uncle Steve, who had arrived in 1940. Many young men, like J.Y. McNabb, enlisted right after Pearl Harbor. Granddaddy, as an older married man with children, was encouraged to find a civilian job that supported the war effort. He did, and in early 1942 he went to work as head of painting at Proctor & Gamble's Gulf Ordinance Plant in Prairie, Mississippi. It was the only time he lived outside Loudon.

Initially, Granddaddy lived in temporary barracks that had been built near the plant. It proved difficult to find a place for the family to live. Prairie was a very small town that had been suddenly over-run by the thousands of people who had come there to work in the ordinance plant. Eventually, he found a room with a bath and two double beds in a house owned by two spinsters. The doors leading into their room were pocket doors; they opened by sliding into the wall on tracks. When closed, the two doors could be locked together with a big skeleton key. Mimi, Granddaddy, and their two young boys would live in this room for three years, until the end of the war in 1945.

East Tennesseans like Granddaddy, Mimi and J.Y. McNabb got to know their own country better because of the war, yet after it most of them chose to come home. They returned with pride, not just in what they had accomplished, but in where they were from. This was a novel thing in East Tennessee. The Civil War and Reconstruction had wounded the pride of the state, but World War II started the process of restoring it. Tennessee, its residents now realized, was a great place to live. Many of those who moved to Oak Ridge agreed. The people were warm and friendly, the weather was nice, and the scenery was beautiful.

That sense of pride endures today. To see it, all you have to do is watch a University of Tennessee Volunteers (Vols) football game. The Vols play at Neyland Stadium in Knoxville, which holds up to 102,455 orange clad fans during home games.[165] If you factor out racing (which is only fair, since cars and horses compete in very different sports), Neyland Stadium is the sixth largest stadium in the world.[166]

In the *world*.

Pride in the University of Tennessee has little to do with the school. Most of the people who go to Vols games never so much as took a class there. Instead, it is pride in East Tennessee. People there love where they live. They wear orange throughout the year, travel thousands of miles for away games, and put signs on their cars and businesses because they are proud of East Tennessee. That civic pride really took hold after World War II, and has remained strong ever since.

Private industry turned the growth from TVA and Oak Ridge into a boom, and Loudon is a perfect example. The Loudon City Council saw farming decline and realized that new jobs were needed. The combination of cheap electricity, the river, the railroad, and nearby Oak Ridge made Loudon well suited for modern industry. The city began offering tax incentives in an effort to attract manufacturing plants.[167] If not for these tax incentives, many lives, including my own, would have been very different.

In 1956, Beth's other grandfather, Ray Birkholz, was working at a Visking manufacturing plant in Chicago. He was offered a promotion to be head of a factory in a place he had never heard of: Loudon, Tennessee. The plant would make hot dog casings, what would later be referred to as "skins for skinless wieners." Loudon was chosen for the new plant because it was a cheap place to do business due to low taxes, cheap electricity, skilled labor, and the railroad. The Loudon City Council had been right. Ray and his wife, Edna, Beth's grandma, lived with their four children in Chicago, but they didn't have to talk long about whether or not Ray should take the job.

"It was a great promotion for him," said Grandma. "And moving south...I'm so glad we did." In the fifteen years I have known her, she has very seldom said that she misses anything up north, other than family. This is typical of the Northern transplants I have met in East Tennessee.

Ray managed the Visking plant as it became operational, and then for years after. Before Visking, Loudon had been home to three manufacturing plants in its history. By the time Bush died, only one was open, the Bacon Creamery, and it employed only twenty or twenty-five people during the week. On weekends, kids would line up outside it to make a few bucks selling ice cream at Loudon football games, but that was very part time. Visking, by contrast, had eight hundred full time employees. As soon as the doors opened, it was, by far, the largest employer in Loudon. The staff was a mix of locals and Northerners, some of whom made the move like Ray Birkholz and others who worked at Oak Ridge. The wages were high, and it was a good job. Later, the plant would be bought by Union Carbide, then by Viskase, which is the name the plant bears today. Everyone in Loudon calls it Visking's, though. They add an 's' but still use the old name.

After Visking's, other plants were built. Manufacturing boomed nationally after World War II, but Loudon benefitted more than most. Staley built a plant to make high fructose corn syrup there. They were bought out by Tate & Lyle years ago, but of course everyone still calls the plant Staley. Uncle Bill worked there for thirty years, until his knees gave out. Maremont built a muffler manufacturing plant. Kimberly-Clark, manufacturer of paper goods, built a plant.

At the end of 2012, there were seventy-three manufacturing, warehousing, transportation and distribution facilities in Loudon County. Manufacturing gave over 4,600 people in Loudon good jobs.[168] In fact, manufacturing was the biggest employer in Tennessee in 2012.[169] It was a drastic change from Bush's life, when most people were subsistence farmers, barely scraping by.

Uncle Larry and Uncle Steve have always loved talking about their childhood in Loudon during the postwar boom. My mother-in-law had plenty of fond memories as well. Granddaddy was working for Speed Queen, selling clothes washers and dryers while Mimi stayed home. Saturday mornings were spent doing chores. Sunday mornings were spent going to church. During the weekday, there was school. When the kids were off from school, whether on weekend afternoons or during the summer, they would leave the house to play and not return until it was time for supper. During the summer, they were often gone all day. Sometimes they might show up for lunch. If they did, they probably had friends with them. If not, they were having lunch at someone else's house. Mimi and the other parents in Loudon didn't keep track of where their kids went or what they were doing. The kids just wandered off to play. If they misbehaved, any adult who saw would correct them. Stores were within walking distance, and kids were often sent to buy groceries. My mother-in-law was sent to the store by her grandmother many times. She bought all kinds of things for her, including cigarettes. It was very different from what Bush knew.

The postwar boom gave a tragic symmetry to Bush's life. Almost to the year, he lived during the worst time in Tennessee history. He was born during the Civil War, which caused Tennessee's decline, and he died just before it recovered. He missed the glory days, before the Civil War, when it gave the nation heroes and presidents, and he missed the boom time, when it was remade. I felt bad for him.

The Birkholzs and others who moved to East Tennessee during the boom blended in with the locals. Beth's dad always felt a fondness for Chicago, including an unfortunate love for the Chicago Cubs baseball team, but Loudon was his home. All of the Birkholz children thought of themselves as local, even though the more established families didn't quite see them that way.

Loudon's new blood and old timers worked, dined, and raised families together. The Birkholz children and the other families that came to Visking's heard the same stories as Uncle Steve and my mother-in-law. They all heard the story of Uncle Bush and his live funeral. It was told over dinner and at work. Fishing buddies would tell it to one another on boats. Neighbors would tell it over tea on front porches. Newspapers occasionally reprinted it, and often ran retrospectives on the anniversary. Bush's story became everyone's story, and a part of everyone's history.

It was a history that grows increasingly distant from daily life. Though the area used to be full of men like Bush, I couldn't find any anymore. Though life changed little during his seventy five years, it is incredibly different as I wrote his story seventy five years later. Even in Cave Creek, farming has declined drastically. People drive farther to work and watch television for entertainment instead of visiting.[170] Telling the story of Bush's live funeral kept history alive, but that history started to be lost in very personal and painful ways.

In 2006, Granddaddy grew ill from a virus making the rounds at the nursing home. Mimi had died five years earlier, after sixty-six years of marriage. After that, it became more and more apparent that Grand-daddy could no longer take care of himself. He moved out of the house he had lived in since 1950, and into the only nursing home in Loudon. It was only a little while later that he fell ill.

Beth went up to see him one last time, but unlike Mimi, he hung on for weeks after everyone had come for that final visit. As the end approached, Beth's mom and uncles took turns sitting with him. Apparently he didn't want them there, because the first time he was alone, he died. It was June 3, 2006. His funeral was done by McGill-Karnes, in the same funeral home in which he and Frank Quinn had first talked to Bush nearly seventy years before. Renee McGill said she was proud to do her best work for him. He was ninety-two years old, and one of the last people alive who had been at the live funeral of Bush Breazeale.

Chapter Ten

The New East Tennessee

In 1996, a year before I met Beth, I took a seminary trip to study ministry in Appalachia. One of our stops was in Kingsport, TN, in the northeast corner of the state. I was staying with a host family, a retired couple. We were seated around the breakfast table watching "Today," which was running down its list of top retirement destinations. Kingsport, TN, was number one. The couple with whom I was staying whooped and hollered like they had just won the lottery. They were so loud I almost fell out of my seat.

In recent years, Tennessee has been consistently rated one of the best places to retire. In May 2013, CNNMoney rated it number one. They specifically recommended East Tennessee because it had "the second lowest cost of living in the country…a low tax burden and great access to medical care."[171] CNN also claimed that Tennessee has a "Florida-like climate." My parents live in Florida, and I can tell you that whoever wrote that clearly hasn't visited both states. Despite this glaring error, Tennessee does have good weather. It's definitely milder than the North. Retirement is such a big business in Tennessee that there is a website called retiretennessee.org, which is part of the Retire Tennessee program, which is in turn part of the Tennessee Department of Economic and Community Development. Retirees are a big part of the new East Tennessee.

A perfect example is Tellico Village.

TVA made plans to build a dam on the Tellico River, but the primary purpose was not to generate electricity. Instead they would build the dam, use eminent domain to seize more land than needed for the reservoir, and sell the excess dry land to developers, to lure wealthy Northerners.[172] It was a land grab, pure and simple. In 1973, those having their land seized tried to stop the dam by filing an endangered species lawsuit on behalf of a tiny fish called the Snail Darter. The case, Tennessee Valley Authority v. Hill, went to the Supreme Court as the first test of the Endangered Species Act. TVA lost, but cut deals and got Congress to amend the Act and create an exemption for the dam. The locals lost their homes. Tellico Dam was finished in 1979 and the seized land around the dam was sold to developers.[173]

Beth's parents tried to buy land in Tellico Village in the late 1980's. They were living overseas at the time and wanted a home to stay in for long stretches when they came home to visit. They were shown a lot and liked it. Then, Beth's mom told the salesman they were actually locals. He went into a back room, and when he returned, he told them that he was sorry, but the lot had been sold. Then he told them there were no other lots for them to see. Today, the homes around Tellico Dam are owned by wealthy, retired Yankees. Beth's mom goes to church there, and loves those Yankees, but they do not blend like Ray and Edna Birkholz and their children.

Suburbanites are the same way. The suburbs that have grown up in East Tennessee over the past several decades are isolated from the people around them. I've lived in several suburbs across the country, and they all have the same culture. Those who moved to suburban Knoxville had more in common with suburbanites outside Chicago, Washington D.C. or Denver than they do with people in Loudon, fifteen miles down the road. Retirees and suburbanites in East Tennessee today spend most of their time around other transplants, rather than those who came during the postwar boom. They don't adopt local history as their own.

Then, there are the tourists.

In 2011, tourism was the second largest industry in Tennessee, which was part of the reason the tax burden was so low.[174] The tourism boom began when Great Smoky Mountains National Park opened in 1934. My cousin, Curt, came all the way from Chicago to honeymoon there. Camping, hiking, and wildlife-viewing are popular activities. The park is home to bear, deer, and even a small population of elk. It is also home to thirty species of salamander, making it the "Salamander Capital of the World."[175] If you really like salamanders, but don't like having to look for them alone, it's probably the happiest place on earth.

Memphis and Nashville are popular, but East Tennessee and Great Smoky Mountains National Park are the heart of Tennessee tourism. Nine million people visit the Smokies every year, triple the number that visit Yosemite or Yellowstone.[176] Two million visit Cades Cove, a valley in the Smokies which tries to preserve frontier Tennessee life, making it the most visited destination in America's most visited national park.[177]

The towns of Sevierville, Pigeon Forge, and Gatlinburg are bustling tourist towns in a line leading into the Smokies. These towns, and their tourist attractions, were built by people whose land was taken for the park. They leveraged their identity as mountain people to create Tennessee-themed attractions and a thriving tourist destination.[178]

Seveirville looks like a mountain version of a tourist town. It's known for its outlet stores, like the Knife Outlet and the Beef Jerky Outlet. Two hundred different kinds of jerky? Awesome! Pigeon Forge is next in line. It looks like a beach town on steroids, only with mountains instead of a beach. It has arcades, go kart tracks, and miniature golf, sandwiched in between crazy places like a huge upside-down mansion and a museum shaped like the bow of the Titanic. I have no idea why someone put a Titanic museum in Pigeon Forge, but then again I feel that way about most things in Pigeon Forge.

I don't feel that way about Dollywood or Gatlinburg. Dolly Parton is a native, and Dollywood is her amusement park in Pigeon Forge. Not only is it fun, but it has a Tennessee mountain feel, and is well worth visiting. Gatlinburg, at the end of the line, also fits well into the mountains. Most of the buildings there are designed to look like a Swiss alpine village.

Others look like rustic cabins or mountain lodges. While Gatlinburg has the most authentic mountain feel, it's also crammed with shops and restaurants. Traffic is horrible in Gatlinburg, and parking is a nightmare, but it, too, is a fun place to visit.

The rest of the state also has plenty to offer. When we visit my mother-in-law, we take I-75 from Chattanooga to Knoxville. On that eighty-mile stretch, we pass exits for Rock City, Ruby Falls, Lake Winnepesaukah Amusement Park, Lookout Mountain, The Lost Sea, Mayfield Dairy, Sweetwater Valley Farm, and The Sequoyah Birthplace Museum. After Bush died, tourism became big business in Tennessee.

The problem is that the tourists don't seem very particular about their history. They love the Hatfield & McCoy Dinner Theater, even though the famous feud took place in West Virginia and Kentucky. That's what the tourists seem to be after: stereotypical hillbilly history, with some humor thrown in. Or they want scenery, roller coasters, and beef jerky. I love beef jerky as much as the next guy, but it makes me sad how neither tourists, nor retirees, nor suburbanites seem to immerse themselves in local history and culture. There are more people in East Tennessee than ever before, but I fear that Bush's story and way of life have never been at greater risk of being lost.

Even people in Loudon and Cave Creek are muddying Bush's story. I heard all kinds of things that research proved wrong. Several different people told me that a woman owned a chest of drawers made out of Bush's coffin, but that wasn't true. There was the story that Bush had been turned down at Kyker Funeral Home in Kingston, though that funeral home hadn't even existed when Bush had his funeral. Quite a few people told me that Bush had gotten into his coffin during the live funeral. Another popular legend was that Bush had given a speech. I don't think any of those things are true, but plenty of people have heard that they happened. The truth becomes muddier over time.

Though Bush is largely remembered as he wanted to be, I do not know that that does much more justice than remembering him as the Boogeyman. Without the murder of Brack Smith, Bush's funeral loses its significance. He should not be remembered for the good nor for the bad, but for both. My fear is that future generations, isolated from local culture, will rush too quickly to celebrate what he did, and in losing sight of why he did it, lose sight of Bush himself. In a

Author, 2010

way, that has already happened, as one final story illustrates.

As Bush became a legend, the Roane County Heritage Commission decided to help preserve his legacy. Sometime in the 1980's or early 1990's, the Commission held a fund raising drive to buy Bush a real gravestone. They raised enough money to put a small, flat monument in the ground on Bush's grave. It is roughly two feet long and twelve inches high, and the inscription had to be abbreviated to fit:

FELIX 'BUSH' BREAZEALE

JUNE 29, 1864

FEB. 9, 1943

HE ATTENDED HIS OWN FUNERAL

JUNE 6, 1938 APPROX. 5 YEARS

BEFORE HE DIED.

After the gravestone was placed, Granddaddy went to see it. Years later, Beth and I were again on his patio when he told us the story.

"I stood there, looking at it," he told us, "and I just knew something wasn't right. I walked down about ten plots, looked down at the ground, and found this lying in the grass." He handed me a metal marker. It was thinner than a license plate, eight inches long and four inches tall. The only printing on it was a grave registration number. Granddaddy said it was the marker from Bush's grave.

I asked Frank Anderson for confirmation. When Frank was a child in the 1950's and 1960's, Decoration

Day was a popular holiday. On that day, people would visit the graves of loved ones and put flowers on them. Decoration Day was originally a day to honor Confederate Civil War dead, but it quickly became the model for Memorial Day. For years, Memorial Day was eschewed in the South in favor of Decoration Day for two reasons. The first is that Memorial Day was thought of as a day when Union dead were honored, and even in East Tennessee, Southerners didn't want to honor Union dead. The other reason is that Decoration Days honored all dead, not just casualties of war. Frank told me that his family would put flowers on graves, sometimes bringing a trunk full. Extended family would sometimes come and have a family reunion. Other times it was just Frank's family placing flowers, telling a few stories, and then leaving.

Because Frank was a frequent visitor to the graves of his family, he knew where Bush had been buried. For years, he had been laying flowers on that grave, with its numbered grave marker. Frank's memory matched Granddaddy's. Bush's headstone is on the wrong grave.

THE END

Acknowledgments

If you aren't one of those people who skip to the end of a book, and you actually read at least the majority of the preceding pages, then you know that it took a lot of people to complete this book. There are so many people to thank that I'm afraid some of them might feel diminished by being on such a lengthy list. I hope that is not the case. Each and every one of you provided vital help and support. This book is as much your accomplishment as it is mine.

First, thanks to my wife Beth. The dedication is true: all the best things in my life come from you. Without you there would be no *Get Low.* My children would have probably been born to some crazy "Jersey Shore" chick with horrible mall hair, and they would definitely not be the awesome people they are. Finally, if not for you, I wouldn't have *you*, and that is something I can barely stand to consider. I love you, Beth. You really are the best.

Next up are the people who helped with the actual writing of the book. It took me several drafts to figure out how to tell this story, and only great friends would wade into such painful pages. Ginger Grunke, Matt Olenn, and Sarah Sambol, you were a tremendous help, not just with assembling the various pieces, but with how to arrange the words on the page. Thank you. Scot Danforth at the University of Tennessee Press, your help with the historical aspects of this story was invaluable. My writing buddy, the incredibly talented Michael Buchanan, wasn't afraid to tell me what was broken, as were George Weinstein and the good folks of the Atlanta Writers Club. You were all inspirational, and the kind of critics everyone needs. Thank you. There are also several people who helped with the publishing. Writing a book is one kind of challenge, but getting it published is entirely another. I'd like to thank Professor Aaron Astor of Maryville College and author Stephen Lyn Bales, both of whom jumped at the chance to help me even though I was a complete stranger. Derrick Eisenhardt and the good folks at Reliquary Press deserve a big thanks for their belief in me, and for their work in taking this from manuscript to published book.

Finally, there are those who helped with the research. Not only were you able to find things that I never would have, you were willing to share them with me. This book could not have happened without any of you. Each of you was vital. Steve Robinson, without you this book would still be just a dream. My mother-in-law, Shari Lillestolen, thank you for hosting me when I needed to do research, even when I didn't bring your grandchildren. And thank you for being so willing to tell a story or find the right person whenever I needed it. Eleanor Barnes, thank you for sharing your story. Bill and Dave Birkholz, you two were always willing to help, and always knew who to talk to. Thank you. Susan Olsen at Woodlawn Cemetery, I appreciate your patient assistance despite my ill timed phone calls.

Rick Holt, thank you for being my research partner and friend. You are awesome. Mick Breazeale, I appreciate all you did, and look forward to our next beer together. Frank Anderson, thank you for sharing so much of your research. Frank Huggins, thank you for telling your family story. I hope you are riding your Harley and enjoying retirement. Don Breazeale, you and your family welcomed me and shared your story, and I thank you all. Harold Amburn, Gene Barrett and Ham Carey, thank you for letting me sit and listen. Ham, special thanks to you for opening your home and sharing your memorabilia. You may be a newcomer, but you sure do know a lot, and your help was vital. Thank you, J.Y. McNabb, for speaking with me, and for sharing your memories. Renee McGill, you are awesome, thank you for all your help. Maybe I can find a way to tell another story about a funeral so we can hang out more.

Three organizations deserve my thanks for their help with my research. If you ever need to research anything about East Tennessee, head over to the East Tennessee Historical Society in Knoxville. Theodore Baehr is a really nice guy who knows that library better than I know my own house, and Sally Polhemus is as helpful as can be. Thank you both. And if you are ever in Kingston, TN, and want to learn more about Bush or the area, be sure to go see the good folks at The Roane County Heritage Commission. Robert Bailey and Darlene Trent really are great people, and they both provided a lot of the material for this book. Thank you both. Finally, the Knoxville News Sentinel newspaper was of vital importance to this book. Paul Efird in particular, thank you. But the whole paper deserves recognition for their ongoing role in telling, and preserving, the stories of East Tennessee. They have my enduring gratitude.

There's one last person to thank. That's you, the reader. Without you, this was all for nothing. So thank you. I hope you enjoyed reading this book as much as I enjoyed writing it for you.

Bibliography

[1] Dunn, Durwood. <u>Cades Cove: A Southern Appalachian Community</u>. University of Tennessee Press, Knoxville. 1988. Pg. 73.

[2] Loudon County Heritage Book Committee, <u>Loudon County, Tennessee and Its People 1870-1999</u>. Walsworth Publishing, Waynesville, NC. 1999. Pg. 1

[3] The Roane County Heritage Commission, *The Old Roane County Courthouse*, <u>www.roanetnheritage.com/courthouse/index.htm</u> (September 21, 2011)

[4] The Museum of Appalachia website, <u>www.museumofappalachia.org</u> (September 21, 2011)

[5] Fowler, Arthur. <u>Early History of Loudon, Tennessee.</u> Presented to the East Tennessee Historical Society, Knoxville, TN. December 2, 1955. Also see note two above.

[6] Gerald Augustus is an expert on the raiding that took place during the war. I interviewed him on May 6, 2014. If you can find a copy of his book, it contains a treasure trove of history of the activity of bushwhackers during the Civil War. Augustus, Gerald. <u>The Loudon County Area of East Tennessee in the War, 1861-1865</u>. Turner Publishing, Nashville, TN. 2000.

[7] Banker, pg. 67-69

[8] Bell, Augusta Grove. <u>Circling Windrock Mountain.</u> Knoxville, TN, University of Tennessee Press. 1998.Pg. 47-73. There is a great description of life in Tennessee right after secession starting on page 47, and a great story about a Confederate general taking reprisal against Union supporters on pg. 55.

[9] Dunn, pg. 25-29. Also Wyatt-Brown, Bertram. <u>Southern Honor: Ethics and Behavior in the Old South.</u> Oxford University Press, New York, NY. 1982. Pg. 30

[10] Dunn, pg. 79-81

[11] This is according to the 1880 census, as found in Eller, Ronald D. <u>Miners, Millhands and Mountaineers: Industrialization of the Appalachian South, 1880-1890</u>. University of Tennessee Press, Knoxville, TN. 1982. pg. 10. Consulting <u>A Supplement to the Statistical Abstract of the United States</u>, Bureau of the Census, 1949, reveals that the number of farms in the United States tripled from two million in 1860 to six million in 1910. Most of these were in the Midwest, where the farms were commercial.

[12] Eller, pg. 17-19. Also Dunn, pg. 75.

[13] There is a great description of the way these small country stores worked in Edward Ayers <u>The Promise of a New South: Life After Reconstruction</u>, Oxford University Press, New York, NY. 2007. pg. 92-94.

[14] Tennessee Blue Book, Tennessee State Division of Publications, Nashville, TN. 2007-08 edition. Section 7: History of Tennessee, page 381. By 1890, hog production in Tennessee had fallen to a third of its 1890 level. See Ayers, Edward L., The Promise of the New South, Life After Reconstruction. Oxford University Press, New York, NY. 2007. Pg. 188.

[15] Dunn, pg. 79 and 182.

[16] Dunn, pg. 29

[17] Bell, page 41.

[18] Professor Halina M. Zaleski from the University of Hawaii has posted a very easy to read summary of hog breeding at http://www2.hawaii.edu/~halina/201/pigb.pdf. Retrieved May 5, 2014.

[19] Eller, pg. 21.

[20] Eller, pg. 7.

[21] Dunn, pg. 29 has a very interesting story about a family recognizing the sound of a family member's gun during a Civil War raid.

[22] Dunn, pg. 74.

[23] Dunn, pg. 77.

[24] Ayers, Edward. Vengeance and Justice: Crime and Punishment in the Eighteenth-Century American South. Oxford University Press, New York, NY. 1985. Pg. 250-262.

[25] Dunn, pg. 71-86.

[26] Ayers, Vengeance, pg. 19-25.

[27] Ayers, Vengeance, pg. 9-15.

[28] Ayers, Vengeance, pg. 264-276.

[29] Ayers, Vengeance, pg. 264.

[30] Prominent positions tended to stay within families. This made it difficult to remove ineffective or dangerous people in government positions. Eller, pg. 30.

[31] Bell, pg. 79.

[32] Wyatt-Brown, pg. 71-72.

[33] Wyatt-Brown, pg. 368.

[34] Ayers, Vengeance, pg. 250-256 and Wyatt-Brown, pg. 436.

[35] Wyatt-Brown, pg. 369-397. For a more detailed example of community justice, read the section called "The Anatomy of a Wife Killing," Ayers, Honor, pg. 485-490.

[36] Ayers, Vengeance, pg. 18.

[37] Interview with Harold Amburn, Gene Barrett, Ham Carey and Steve Robinson. April 25, 2014.

[38] Dunn, pg. 40.

[39] The Knoxville Journal, "Livest Corpse You Ever Saw to Attend Own Funeral Today," Sunday, June 26, 1938, page 1.

[40] Adkisson, C.W., "Aged Roane County Farmer Gives Reasons for His 'Funeral' Today," Chattanooga Times, June 25, 1938, pg. 7.

[41] Adkisson, "Aged Roane County Farmer Gives Reasons for His 'Funeral' Today," pg. 6.

[42] Dunn, pg. 34-28 and Eller, pg. 25-28.

[43] Dunn, pg. 79.

[44] Eller, pg. 7.

45 Fowler, Arthur, Early History of Loudon, Tennessee, Before the East Tennessee Historical Society at Knoxville, TN, on December 2, 1955. Rhea Alexander Collection, McClung Library, Knoxville, TN.

[46] Ibid.

[47] Thirteenth Census of the United States, 1913, United States Bureau of the Census, Washington D.C.

[48] Eller, pg. XX and 225-230.

[49] Ayers, Promise, pg. 213.

[50] Ayers, Honor, pg. 193.

[51] Current Population Reports, Estimates of Illiteracy by States: 1960. United States Census Bureau. Feb. 12, 1963.

[52] Whisnant, David, All That Is Native and Fine: The Politics of Culture in an American Region. University of North Carolina Press, Chapel Hill, NC. 1983. Pg. 110.

[53] Ibid.

[54] Ayers, Promise, pg. 32-33 and 342

[55] Blackberry Farm website, www.blackberryfarm.com (September 21, 2011)

[56] Eller, pg. 19.

[57] Ayers, Promise, pg. 311-313.

[58] Knoxville News-Sentinel, "Aged Man to Hear His Own Funeral," May 1, 1938, page 4.

[59] Adkisson, "Aged Roane County Farmer Gives Reasons for His 'Funeral' Today," pg. 7.

[60] Ibid.

[61] Eller, pg. 22.

[62] Ayers, Honor, pg. 278.

[63] Bell, pg. 93.

[64] There is a great section about the divisiveness of Prohibition in Ayers, Promise, pg. 178-182.

[65] Ibid.

[66] Dunn, pg. 110.

[67] McCauley, Deborah Vansau, Appalachian Mountain Religion: A History, University of Illinois Press, Urbana and Chicago, 1995. Pg. 97-150.

[68] Ibid, and Ayers, Promise, pg. 161.

[69] Ibid.

[70] Dunn, pg. 193 and Wyatt-Brown, pg. 55.

[71] Sexual double standards are covered in detail in Wyatt-Brown, pg. 293-295.

[72] Dunn, pg. 194 discusses in more detail how those who kept the consumption of alcohol quiet avoided punishment.

[73] Wyatt-Brown, pg. 205.

[74] Adkisson, Aged Roane County Farmer Gives Reasons for His 'Funeral' Today, pg. 7.

[75] Wyatt-Brown, pg. 329.

[76] Wyatt-Brown, pg. 34.

[77] Clan Breazeale website, www.clanbreazeale.com, (November 29, 2011)

[78] Dunn, pg. 191.

[79] For more about the unique status of ministers in the community, see Dunn, pg. 111.

[80] Adkisson, Aged Roane County Farmer Gives Reasons for his 'Funeral' Today, pg. 7.

[81] *Knoxville News-Sentinel*, "Casket Began Here," June 27, 1938, page 1.

[82] The Knoxville Journal, "Livest Corpse You Ever Saw to Attend Own Funeral Today," page 4.

[83] Interview with Harold Amburn, Gene Barrett, Ham Carey and Steve Robinson. April 25, 2014.

[84] Kiesel, Kenneth. Dayton Aviation: The Wright Brothers to McCook Field, Arcadia Publishing, Mount Pleasant, SC. 2012.

[85] Dunn, pg. 192.

[86] Ibid.

[87] Ogden, A.W. Loudon Has Electric Show Place, The Knoxville News-Sentinel, Knoxville, TN. April 7, 1935.

[88] Historic Tennessee Theatre, www.tennesseetheatre.com (September 21, 2011)

[89] The Tennessee Encyclopedia of History and Culture, http://tennesseeencyclopedia.net/entry.php?rec=1526 (November 25, 2012)

[90] For more about funerals as social gatherings, see Eller, pg. 35.

[91] Frank Anderson interview. July 8, 2011.

[92] Dunn, pg. 191.

[93] Ibid.

[94] The Knoxville News-Sentinel, "Undertaker Ready for 'Live Corpse'", June 24, 1938.

[95] The Knoxville News-Sentinel, "Bush Talks to Preacher for his 'Funeral'", June 25, 1938.

[96] Adkisson, "Aged Roane County Farmer Gives Reasons for His 'Funeral' Today," pg. 7.

[97] Bonnie Tom Robinson, "'Bush' Breazeale Goes Back to Farm Happy After His 'Buryin' That Went Off So Nice," *Knoxville News-Sentinel*, June 27, 1938, page 1.

[98] Robinson, "'Bush' Breazeale Goes Back to Farm Happy After His 'Buryin' That Went Off So Nice," page 2.

[99] Robinson, "'Bush' Breazeale Goes Back to Farm Happy After His 'Buryin' That Went Off So Nice," page 2.

[100] Robinson, "'Bush' Breazeale Goes Back to Farm Happy After His 'Buryin' That Went Off So Nice," page 2.

[101] Robinson, "'Bush' Breazeale Goes Back to Farm Happy After His 'Buryin' That Went Off So Nice," page 2.

[102] Robinson, "'Bush' Breazeale Goes Back to Farm Happy After His 'Buryin' That Went Off So Nice," page 2.

[103] The Roane County News, "Roane's Most Publicized 'Funeral' Recalled." Kingston, TN. April 5, 1973.

[104] Robinson, "'Bush' Breazeale Goes Back to Farm Happy After His 'Buryin' That Went Off So Nice," page 2.

[105] Robinson, "'Bush' Breazeale Goes Back to Farm Happy After His 'Buryin' That Went Off So Nice," page 2.

[106] Robinson, "'Bush' Breazeale Goes Back to Farm Happy After His 'Buryin' That Went Off So Nice," page 2.

[107] Robinson, "'Bush' Breazeale Goes Back to Farm Happy After His 'Buryin' That Went Off So Nice," page 2.

[108] Robinson, "'Bush' Breazeale Goes Back to Farm Happy After His 'Buryin' That Went Off So Nice," page 1.

[109] Robinson, "'Bush' Breazeale Goes Back to Farm Happy After His 'Buryin' That Went Off So Nice," page 2.

[110] Barney Ballard, "8,000 at 'Funeral' Service for Live 'Corpse,', The Knoxville Journal, Knoxville, TN. June 27, 1938, page 1.

[111] Rick Holt interview

[112] Robinson, "'Bush' Breazeale Goes Back to Farm Happy After His 'Buryin' That Went Off So Nice," page 2.

[113] The Roane County News, "Roane's Most Publicized 'Funeral' Recalled." April 5, 1973.

[114] Dwight D. Eisenhower Presidential Library and Museum, "The 1919 Transcontinental Motor Convoy," http://www.eisenhower.archives.gov/research/online_documents/1919_convoy.html. (November 30, 2012).

[115] Frank Anderson interview. July 8, 2011.

[116] Robinson, "'Bush' Breazeale Goes Back to Farm Happy After His 'Buryin' That Went Off So Nice," page 2.

[117] For more about the Tennessee perspective on the Scopes Trial, see Banker, pg. 156-159.

[118] Robinson, "'Bush' Breazeale Goes Back to Farm Happy After His 'Buryin' That Went Off So Nice," page 2.

[119] Robinson, "'Bush' Breazeale Goes Back to Farm Happy After His 'Buryin' That Went Off So Nice," page 2.

[120] Robinson, "'Bush' Breazeale Goes Back to Farm Happy After His 'Buryin' That Went Off So Nice," page 2.

[121] The Roane County News, "Roane's Most Publicized 'Funeral' Recalled." April 5, 1973.

[122] Robinson, "'Bush' Breazeale Goes Back to Farm Happy After His 'Buryin' That Went Off So Nice," page 2.

[123] Robinson, "'Bush' Breazeale Goes Back to Farm Happy After His 'Buryin' That Went Off So Nice," page 2.

[124] Robinson, "'Bush' Breazeale Goes Back to Farm Happy After His 'Buryin' That Went Off So Nice," page 2.

[125] Robinson, "'Bush' Breazeale Goes Back to Farm Happy After His 'Buryin' That Went Off So Nice," page 2.

[126] Frank Anderson interview. July 8, 2011.

[127] Robinson, "'Bush' Breazeale Goes Back to Farm Happy After His 'Buryin' That Went Off So Nice," page 2.

[128] Robinson, "'Bush' Breazeale Goes Back to Farm Happy After His 'Buryin' That Went Off So Nice," page 2.

[129] The Roane County News, "Roane's Most Publicized 'Funeral' Recalled." April 5, 1973.

[130] The Roane County News, "Roane's Most Publicized 'Funeral' Recalled." April 5, 1973.

[131] Barney Ballard, "8,000 at 'Funeral' Service for Live 'Corpse,', *The Knoxville Journal*, Knoxville, TN. June 27, 1938, page 2.

[132] Robinson, "'Bush' Breazeale Goes Back to Farm Happy After His 'Buryin' That Went Off So Nice," page 2.

[133] Robinson, "'Bush' Breazeale Goes Back to Farm Happy After His 'Buryin' That Went Off So Nice," page 2.

[134] Robinson, "'Bush' Breazeale Goes Back to Farm Happy After His 'Buryin' That Went Off So Nice," page 2.

[135] Robinson, "'Bush' Breazeale Goes Back to Farm Happy After His 'Buryin' That Went Off So Nice," page 2.

[136] The Roane County News, "Roane's Most Publicized 'Funeral' Recalled." April 5, 1973.

[137] The Roane County News, "Roane's Most Publicized 'Funeral' Recalled." April 5, 1973.

[138] Robinson, "'Bush' Breazeale Goes Back to Farm Happy After His 'Buryin' That Went Off So Nice," page 2.

[139] *The Knoxville News-Sentinel*, "Happy 'Body' Looks at Crowd from Hearse," June 27, 1938, page 1.

[140] *The Knoxville Journal*, June 27, 1938, page 2.

[141] Leslie Hart, "Crowd Lauds Funeral Idea," *The Knoxville Journal*, June 27, 1938, page 1.

[142] Leslie Hart, "Crowd Lauds Funeral Idea," page 2.

[143] Leslie Hart, "Crowd Lauds Funeral Idea," page 2.

[144] Leslie Hart, "Crowd Lauds Funeral Idea," page 2.

[145] Leslie Hart, "Crowd Lauds Funeral Idea," page 2.

[146] Leslie Hart, "Crowd Lauds Funeral Idea," page 2.

[147] Leslie Hart, "Crowd Lauds Funeral Idea," page 2.

[148] Leslie Hart, "Crowd Lauds Funeral Idea," page 2.

[149] Clan Breazeale website, *Uncle Bush Goes to New York City for Ripley's Believe It or Not Radio Program,* http://www.clanbreazeale.com/UncleBush/BushRipleyNYCtrip.htm (November 29, 2011)

[150] Clara Childress interview.

[151] Frank Anderson interview, July 8, 2011.

[152] Ibid.

[153] Ibid.

[154] Taylor, A.J.P. *The Second World War and its Aftermath.* Folio Society (Vol 4 of 4), 1998. pg. 142.

[155] Willmott, H.P. *The Barrier and the Javelin: Japanese and Allied Pacific Strategies: February to June 1942.* Annapolis, MD: Naval Institute Press. 2008. Pp. 522-523

[156] Oak Ridge National Laboratory, *Swords to Plowshares: A Short History of Oak Ridge National Laboratory (1943-1993).* http://web.ornl.gov/info/swords/swords.shtml   Retrieved Oct. 1, 2013

[157] Tennessee Valley Authority, *From the New Deal to a New Century,* http://www.tva.com/abouttva/history.htm. Retrieved Oct. 1, 2013

[158] United States Census Bureau, *Labor Report,* http://www2.census.gov/prod2/statcomp/documents/CT1970p1-05.pdf. Page 17, column 127. Retrieved Sept. 30, 2013

[159] Tennessee Valley Authority, *From the New Deal to a New Century*

[160] Plater, Zygmund, The Snail Darter and the Dam, How Pork Barrel Politics Endangered a Little Fish and Killed a River. Yale University Press, New Haven, CN, 2013. Kindle version. Loc. 323-367.

[161] Ayers, Promise, pg. 73.

[162] Nothingbutnets.net, *Saving Lives,* http://www.nothingbutnets.net/new/saving-lives/. Retrieved Oct. 5, 2013

[163] Centers for Disease Control and Prevention, *The History of Malaria, an Ancient Disease,* http://www.cdc.gov/malaria/about/history/. Retrieved Oct. 1, 2013.

[164] Wikipedia, *Oak Ridge, Tennessee.* http://en.wikipedia.org/wiki/Oak_Ridge,_Tennessee. Retrieved Oct. 1, 2013.

[165] University of Tennessee Sports, *Neyland Stadium,* http://www.utsports.com/facilities/neyland_stadium.html. Retrieved Oct. 1, 2013.

[166] Wikipedia, *List of Stadiums by Capacity,* http://en.wikipedia.org/wiki/List_of_stadiums_by_capacity. Retrieved Oct. 1, 2013

[167] Interview with Harold Amburn, Gene Barrett, Ham Carey and Steve Robinson. April 25, 2014

[168] Loudon County Economic Development Agency, "Existing Industry Directory, Loudon, Tennessee." June 30, 2013

[169] National Associating of Manufacturers, *Tennessee Manufacturing Facts,* http://www.nam.org/~/media/125F53C48B1C40D291A4DD35B9AFD215.ashx.Retrieved Oct. 2, 2013

[170] Eleanor Barnes interview, April 26, 2014.

[171] CNNMoney, *Best states for retirement aren't what you may think,* http://money.cnn.com/2013/05/06/retirement/best-states/index.html Retrieved Oct. 1, 2013

[172] Plater, Zygmund, <u>The Snail Darter and the Dam, How Pork Barrel Politics Endangered a Little Fish and Killed a River</u>. Yale University Press, New Haven, CN, 2013. Kindle version. Loc. 323-367.

[173] Plater, loc. 1736-5977.

[174] TNReport, *Tourism's Economic Impact Up 6.3% in Volunteer State,* http://tnreport.com/2011/10/07/tourisms-economic-impact-up-6-3-in-volunteer-state/. Retrieved Oct. 2, 2013

[175] History.com, *Tennessee,* http://www.history.com/topics/tennessee, Retrieved Oct. 1, 2013

[176] VisitMySmokies.com, *The Great Smoky Mountains National Park,* http://www.visitmysmokies.com/great-smoky-mountains-national-park/. Retrieved Oct. 2, 2013

[177] Dunn writes magnificently about the end of Cades Cove. I highly recommend reading his book.

[178] Banker, pg. 174-177 describes how this happened in more detail.

CPSIA information can be obtained at www.ICGtesting.com
Printed in the USA
LVOW06s0809270715

447760LV00001B/34/P